you&your

Range Rover

you&your

Range Rover

Dave Pollard *Buying, enjoying, maintaining, modifying*

M269 CVC

First published in January 2004

A catalogue record for this book is available from the British Library

ISBN 1 85960 617 2

Library of Congress catalog card no. 2003113467

Published by Haynes Publishing, Sparkford, Yeovil, Somerset, BA22 7JJ, UK
Tel: 01963 442030 Fax: 01963 440001
Int. tel: +44 1963 442030 Int. fax: +44 1963 440001
E-mail: sales@haynes.co.uk
Web site: www.haynes.co.uk

Haynes North America, Inc.,
861 Lawrence Drive, Newbury Park,
California 91320, USA

Printed and bound in England by J. H. Haynes & Co. Ltd, Sparkford

Contents

Acknowledgements

Thanks of course to everyone involved in the production of this book, notably the following companies/individuals who were pivotal in supplying equipment, information and photographs or photographic opportunities: Car Parts Direct (Mark Cornwall), Eberspächer pre-heaters (John Jennings), Gaydon Heritage Motor Centre (Anders Clausager), Iwema Enterprise, (Hugo Van Osch and Gordon Finlay), Goodyear GB Ltd (Ron Pike), Land Rover UK, M.A.D. Suspension (Clive Berry and Wim Nells), McDonalds Land Rover Limited (Rupert Astbury and Andy McDonald), MetaSystem UK Ltd (Victoria Nicod and Martine Layland), David Mitchell's Landcraft, Nationwide Trim (Trevor Edwards), Paddock Spares, Pharmhouse Marketing (Mark Adams), Polybush UK (Ian Dicken), Rimmer Bros (Graham Rimmer, Bill Rimmer, Piers Philo), RPi Engineering (Chris Crane and Holly Hollingdale), and Teng Tools Ltd (Colin North).

Unless otherwise credited, all the photographs in this book are either my own or the property of Land Rover UK Limited. A special thanks, however, to Nick Dimbleby for some truly stunning shots, particularly of the Series 3 Range Rover.

Dave Pollard,
Oswestry,
November 2003

Author's notes:

The name 'Land Rover' always had a hyphen until the early 1980s, but for the sake of simplicity and consistency, it is used throughout this book without the hyphen.

Please note that all photographs showing vehicles off-road were taken either on official off-road routes, purpose-made off-road centres or on private land with the owners' permission.

Introduction – nobody does it better

Land Rover's press hype about the latest Series 3 Range Rover described it as 'the most capable vehicle in the world'. Those of us who already own a Range Rover – even if it's not the latest £65,000 hi-tech marvel – have known this for some time. It's a car that can crawl around in a muddy farmyard pulling a 2-tonne trailer of hay one day then take five folks and their luggage for a weekend at Le Mans the next day without breaking its stride or, importantly, looking remotely out of place.

In totally practical terms, there's lots of space behind the rear seat and it's easy to load-up because of the excellent, horizontally split rear tailgate. Of course, those with later, more luxuriously kitted cars will probably be a bit reluctant to start chucking bales of hay in the back. But when you've got such an excellent tow car, all you need is a trailer and you're away, Dobbin's feed delivery is assured. Caravaner's love them for the same reason and if reversing a trailer is one of the more difficult motoring manoeuvres you'll come across, using the Range Rover's low-ratio gearbox when doing this, makes life so much easier.

Inside, it is comfortable for five adults and it can easily keep up with the push and shove of modern traffic (although early carburettor cars make harder going of it than fuel-injected models). The oft-mentioned lofty driving position makes it fun to drive and safe, too, because you can see 'through' corners and over hedges in the country, and over the tops of traffic in motorway situations.

It's a big bonus, too, for children, who just love looking down on the world. Even with a basic specification, it is a pleasant environment, and from the late 1980s onwards, even 'basic' meant very well equipped indeed.

As if this weren't enough, its off-road abilities are staggering, despite often being overlooked in favour of Land Rover's other, more down-to-earth products. At the end of the day, the Defender range and the S1/S2 Discovery were basically rebodied S1/S2 Range Rovers. Even with road tyres, it is impressive in muddy, slippery situations, and with a set of good MT (mud-terrain) tyres, it will climb hills you could hang glide off! If you really get the bug, you can invest in a few reprints of some of the clever Range Rover ads of the past; who can forget the Rangie ploughing through a deep ford, and the strap line: 'I brake for fish'?

Fuel costs are undoubtedly a drawback though, with diesel engines typically returning between 22mpg and 30mpg, the latter requiring a long journey with a gentle right foot. The V8's thirst is less impressive, getting better as advanced technology and electronics took over the job of fuel measurement. As an average, expect around 15mpg.

An increasing number of owners (present company included) have taken the LPG route, thus retaining the superb V8 engine but running it on virtually half-price fuel. My own 1990, 3.9-litre automatic gives just under 20mpg on a steady motorway cruise, when running on petrol. Later cars than this should be able to crack 22/23mpg on similar runs but remember, that if you do a little off-roading, or even some snow-bound road work, your mpg will easily plummet into single figures.

DID YOU KNOW?

The underpinnings of the Classic Range Rover – ladder chassis, suspension layout, gearbox/engine etc. – are basically the same for the Discovery, 90/110 and Defender models.

The rustic timbered house in the country, with gravelled driveway, needed a Range Rover to complete the picture. By 1981, Land Rover had zeroed in on the target market. (Nick Dimbleby)

Most owners never use the off-road abilities, the low box, its towing capacity or anything much other than its ability to sweep up and down the motorways in safe and comfortable ease. For my own part, I do a fair bit of the latter, but in addition, it has been used as a base for some very necessary tree lopping (where the fold-down lower tailgate got us to the right height for some chainsawing), towed two halves of a park home down lanes barely wide enough for the car and, literally, ploughed along snowbound, narrow mountain lanes in low-box second gear with aplomb.

That's not to say the Range Rover is perfect, far

from it in fact; the build quality has long been a bone of contention and they suffer badly from rust. So, despite its dynamic abilities, there must be another reason for Range Rover enthusiasm. Owners of Japanese 4x4s in particular often beat on about the reliability and build-quality of their chosen steeds, something which is undeniable, and question the wisdom of my owning a 13-year-old Rangie. So what tips the scales? The cost of spares. Having replaced a fuel tank on my '79 model for just £100, I was well pleased. A colleague with an Oriental version of this English classic was charged £850 – and lo, I was even more pleased! The massive availability and choice of spares and accessories is a very definite plus point when it comes to owning and maintaining a Range Rover.

Chapter One

Pre-history

Land Rover is, today, the company behind the 'Best 4x4s by far', but originally, the company was Rover and the product, a Land Rover, was just one of the vehicles it produced. The Range Rover and Land Rover heritages are inextricably linked in a story which starts just after the Second World War. In terms of manufacturing production, this period was particularly difficult, not least because steel production was very limited. In order to encourage export, the government offered incentives in the form of extra steel allowance for those who used up some of the aluminium surplus. The managing director of Rover at that time was Spencer Wilks, and while he

wrestled with this seemingly insoluble problem, his brother Maurice had problems of his own. He had a 250-acre farm on the Isle of Anglesey and there was only one vehicle capable of getting him around the varied terrain – a wartime Wilys General Purpose Vehicle (shortened to GP, and thence to Jeep). As it neared the end of its useful life, Maurice had to consider its replacement; he had

It is hard to credit perhaps, but this 80-inch Series 1 Land Rover is – in essence at least – a very close relative to the Range Rover, with its ladder chassis, Birmabright bodywork and four-wheel drive. (Nick Dimbleby)

Even 30-odd years after it was first launched, this Land Rover, now
designated Series III, had barely changed in appearance.

almost come to the conclusion that another Jeep was the
only answer when it dawned on him that this huge gap
in the market could be manna from heaven for Rover.

Both Maurice and Spencer saw immediately the
potential in building a 'British Jeep' and started working
on the project straight away. At a board meeting in
1947, they were able to show a working prototype. They
told the board that the Land Rover (the name had
already been decided) would use a Rover P3 engine,
gearbox and back axle and that there would be no need
for expensive body dies – the entire body would be
made from aluminium.

Built in the summer of 1947, all the early prototypes
had a tractor-like centrally mounted steering wheel.
This novel idea was to save time and money by avoiding
having to build RHD and LHD cars for different export
markets. By the time the Land Rover was in production
this had been dropped, but the idea that one of the
original vehicles still exists somewhere, crops up again
and again.

The basic guidelines used for its development leaned
heavily on its usefulness to the farming community; it
had to go anywhere a tractor could and have a power
take-off to enable it to use a range of existing farm
machinery. A range of bolt-on accessories would
further enhance its appeal. This thinking was also
applied when considering export sales, and the car was
put forward as the vehicle to tackle everything from
harsh deserts to dense jungles and just about
everything in between.

The debut

It was only one year after the concept was first aired
that the Land Rover was shown to the public. It featured
the 50bhp 1,595cc engine as used in the Rover P3.
Its 80in wheelbase was exactly the same as the Wilys
Jeep and other similarities included the separate box-
section chassis frame with a front-mounted
engine/gearbox with transfer box at the rear driving
propeller shafts to the front and rear live axles.
Suspension comprised telescopic dampers and semi-
elliptic (cart) springs. Because of cost restrictions, the
chassis sections were made from four strips of sheet

steel welded together to make the square-section 'boxes'. To save the cost of expensive tooling-up, aluminium body panels were used.

The press and public alike were ecstatic and so began a story of British off-road, 4WD vehicles that has continued for over 50 years and shows no sign of slowing down. The original production run was to have been 1,000 units per year – a figure restricted by the government. After arguing that the Land Rover could have a successful future as an export vehicle, the production was increased. In fact, in the first year of production, a staggering 8,000 Land Rovers rolled off the assembly lines and by 1951, Land Rovers were out-selling Rover cars by a factor of two to one!

The Series cars

Over the years, Land Rover has consistently changed the specification, occasionally launching 'new' models, but never straying far from the original 'go-anywhere, do-anything' concept that was so right in 1948. The engine sizes were gradually increased, petrol and diesel options were offered and both six-cylinder and V8 options were available at various times. The wheelbase grew steadily longer and seating arrangements varied from two men plus load to the equivalent of small coach parties! But right up to its

demise in 1985, the Land Rover was always recognisable as such; moreover, the very last car off the production line was clearly a close relative of the first model to hit the streets.

	Wheelbase (inches)	Produced From	To
Series I	80	1948	1954
	86	1954	1956
	88	1957	1958
	107	1955	1958
	109	1957	1958
Series II		1958	1961
	109	1962	1971
Series IIA	88	1962	1971
	109	1962	1971
Series III	88	1972	1984
	109	1972	1984
	109 V8	1979	1985

In 1983/84, the Land Rover 110 and 90 ranges were introduced, the first models to make use of the basic Range Rover chassis and underpinnings. The longer, more practical 110 was the workhorse whereas the shorter 90 . . .

... was the shining star. Its proportions made it easier on the eye (reflected in the residual values) and with little in the way of front/rear overhang, its off-road abilities were awesome. As Land Rover sought to separate the manufacturing company from its products, both models were badged Defenders, as here. (Nick Dimbleby)

Refining the Land Rover – the 90, 110 and Defender

As we shall see, everything changed in 1970 with the launch of the drastically different Range Rover. But there was still a huge market for those who actually needed a tough, no-frills four-wheel-drive machine and it was clear that as the '70s came to a close, the Land Rover strangle-hold on the market had been weakened considerably. Competition, particularly from Japanese companies such as Mitsubishi, Toyota and Daihatsu was fierce; the products were tough, reliable and, more importantly, modern and comfortable. No longer was it necessary for a working vehicle to be hard work in itself.

So, in 1983, Land Rover chose the Geneva Motor Show for the launch of the replacement for its epony-mous, go-anywhere 4x4; and not without some serious trepidation. They faced the problem of bringing what was essentially a 30-year-old design right up-to-date, but in a way that didn't alienate the existing clientele. First off the blocks was the 110 model, which followed the tradition of naming models after the (approximate) wheelbase length – in inches of course – the Land Rover

'2794mm' wouldn't have quite the same ring to it! To a great extent, the 90 and 110 were essentially rebodied Range Rovers. Look underneath and you will see a remarkably similar ladder chassis, damper/spring arrangement, gearbox/engine combination etc. Compared to the S3 Land Rover, the 110 had a higher, single-piece windscreen, wider track, more comfortable seats, wind-up windows, modern interior trim, 'trendy' wheel arch extensions and even an air conditioning option. But even from across the street, it was from all angles unmistakably a Land Rover and was immediately accepted. The first engine line-up was a choice of the familiar 2¼-litre petrol and diesel engines, although the diesel became 2.5 litres in 1985 and was turbocharged the following year to help it keep up with the opposition. The ubiquitous V8 engine was also available. The four-cylinder cars were fitted with a five-speed gearbox.

In 1984, the three-door version, the '90', arrived on the scene and this proved to be even more popular, especially with hardened off-roaders, who relished the lack of overhang at either end which enabled them to drive to areas previously the sole reserve of mountain goats. A real treat was the introduction in 1985 of the V8 option in the 90 – which was fine, as long as you had shares in BP!

In September 1990, the 90 and 110 models both became 'Defenders' with minor modifications here and

there and a major engine–bay improvement with the installation of the 200 TDi diesel engine, a great improvement on the increasingly outdated units fitted since its launch. In 1994, the Defenders kept in line with other Land Rover products as the 200 TDi unit was phased out, making way for the 300 TDi version. At the same time, the tougher R380 manual five-speed gearbox was fitted.

Land Rover were not only happy to have replaced what seemed irreplaceable, but also that they had done it using parts-bin technology. So, this was not only successful but relatively cheap to produce, too. As we shall see in Chapter Two, this idea was to prove itself again, with another Land Rover vehicle: have a guess at which one . . .?

Discovering new markets

By the end of the 1980s, the Defenders had pulled back the ground they had lost with the Series I–III cars and the Range Rover was continuing to annexe upmarket 4x4 sales. But there was a gap in-between the two sectors, a niche market for mid-range 'lifestyle' 4x4s which was being ruthlessly – and profitably exploited by the Japanese manufacturers. Land Rover had to retaliate, but with cashflow rather limited, the options were few. Most of the opposition were able to offer a long and short wheelbase version of the same car, something that was

Launched in 1989, the Discovery was dropped into the space between the luxury Range Rover and the work-a-day Defenders. Few people would link the three, other than via the Land Rover badge, but like the Land Rovers, beneath the aluminium skin is – yes, a Range Rover.

not on the cards for Land Rover. The then MD formed a team called the Swift Group to solve the problem, the project name for the new car being Jay. First off, they needed to address the size – with two wheelbase options being out of the question, they decided on a compromise which fell between the short Defender 90 and the longer Defender 110 – clearly, the Range Rover's 100in wheelbase was ideal. And by using the chassis and underpinnings (axles, drivetrain and suspension) etc., the company saved an awful lot of time and not a little cash. One major difference when looking under the car was that the Boge self-levelling suspension was not fitted to the Discovery. It added complexity and cost and the engineers thought it simpler just to beef up the rear springs to compensate. Anyone who has ever had to purchase a replacement Boge unit will agree with their thinking on this point.

However, being Range Rover-based brought its own problems, because the new vehicle had to be pitched into a totally different market to the older car and be seen as nothing like its bigger brother. It succeeded so well that most owners don't realise that the Series 1

Left: The 'eyes have it' – the 2003 model Discovery still retained plenty of Range Rover heritage; just check out the headlamps and compare it to the Series 3 car for confirmation.

Below left: The Range Rover proved to be a huge sales success, incredibly competent on and off-road and a style icon to boot (it has been exhibited in the Louvre museum in Paris as a work of automotive art). During its 26-year span, it changed from a semi-working tool for the rich farmer to a luxury carriage for those, literally, wanting to rise above the herd. That said, from the outside, it changed very little . . . (Nick Dimbleby)

Discovery is in fact longer, taller and heavier than the car on which it is based! The roof height at the rear was made necessary by the need to make plenty of headroom for those passengers in the 'boot', sitting on the pull-down side seats. The stepped rear roof line could have been just another Daihatsu copy (the Fourtrak already had this feature) but Land Rover made it individual by including a roof light at either side. Apart from looking good from the outside, it also had the effect of making the cabin feel particularly spacious

. . . as we can see on this 1990 model.

and airy. Because it was now higher than the Range Rover, it was decided to try an optical illusion – cutting off the rear of the car sharply (compare with the Range Rover's angled back), not only disguised the height but made the Discovery look shorter, too. The extra height meant that the roof had to be steel in order to give some extra structural strength to the taller car, unlike the Range Rover, where the roof was aluminium. The company also raided the corporate parts bin, sourcing the door handles from the Morris Marina, headlamps from the Sherpa van and tail lamps from the Maestro van. Inside, there was plenty of competition among designers, but it was '80s style gurus, Conran Design that won out in the end, although Land Rover's own design team did have some input. The need to attract the young, 'lifestyle' customer with a bright and airy interior was the prime consideration and to get away from the more 'serious' interior of the Range Rover.

As a rule, designing and building a vehicle from scratch takes a long time, but not in this case. From its conception in 1986, it was just two and a half years before the wraps were removed and the Discovery was shown to an impressed motoring public on 12 September 1989 at the Frankfurt Motor Show.

From barn to boardroom – the Series 1

An upmarket 4WD vehicle had been on the Land Rover stocks twenty years before the Range Rover went on sale. The company built a few special prototypes in the Fifties and between 1951 and 1959 some 23 so-called 'Road Rovers' were produced in two basic styles, nearly all of them two-wheel drive. With hesitation, which came to epitomise the UK car industry, Rover found itself unsure as to its exact target market and as a result, dropped the project only a short while before production was scheduled to begin. One of the main stumbling blocks was the lack of a really suitable engine but, as with the Land Rover concept itself, inspiration was soon to wing its way across the Atlantic.

The original Land Rover took much of its inspiration from the American Wilys Jeep and as the 'leisure utility' market boomed in the USA throughout the 1960s, the leaders of that particular pack (Chevrolet's Blazer and Ford's Bronco) were to inspire the Range Rover. Given the high specification and the huge, reliable and powerful engines, it is not surprising that Land Rover was having trouble selling its slow and utilitarian

Opposite: Even after the launch of its successor in 1994, the S1 Range Rover was still the weapon of choice for many on the Croisière Blanche event, which takes place in the French Alps. (Nick Dimbleby)

Below: Mark Clark has restored this very early model faithfully, to give us some idea of how life was in the early 1970s. Note the Rostyle steel wheels (only 6in wide, as opposed to the 7in-wide Vogue wheels), lack of vinyl trim on the 'D' pillars, silver-painted bumpers and bonnet-mounted wing mirrors. But other than relatively minor points, the car still looks smooth and stylish and many still regard the two-door model as being better proportioned. (Mark Clark)

This interesting body-less model at the Motor Heritage Centre, shows the simplicity of the basic design. (Nick Dimbleby)

products in America. Charles Spencer (Spen) King was in charge of the New Vehicle Projects department at Rover and, having worked on the Rover 2000 and, in the 1950s, on the gas turbine car, was no stranger to pushing back a few boundaries. Working with him was Gordon Bashford, already a Rover veteran of 30 years, and stylist David Bache. Gordon had designed the chassis for every Rover and Land Rover vehicle produced in that time so between them, they formed a formidable partnership and one which found itself examining the prospect of producing Land Rover's own 'leisure utility' vehicle under the code name 'Oyster'.

Their initial proposals in 1966 included a coil spring and damper arrangement (for a more comfortable road ride and better off-road axle articulation) and power from the six-cylinder Rover unit. However, the latter was soon ditched in favour of the more powerful and torquey V8 'Buick' engine to which Rover had acquired the rights. The 'new' car was planned with 4WD, based on a ladder chassis but with disc brakes all-round to cope with the anticipated increase in performance.

The 100-inch Station Wagon

Tests, experiments and much debate followed and by 1967, plenty had been decided about the vehicle, now dubbed the '100-inch Station Wagon' – the wheelbase dimension in inches was the traditional way to name a Land Rover and so it carried on here. To meet strict US crash regulations, the immensely strong ladder chassis was to have a steel skeleton body, and the unstressed outer panels were to be of aluminium – or more accurately, Birmabright (like the Land Rover). Considering future export markets, many of which required vehicles to be supplied in CKD (completely knocked down, i.e. kit) form, the car was designed to be built almost like a productionised kit-car. Proposals for a more downmarket model, equipped with a four-cylinder engine were thankfully scrapped in 1968. (Land Rover enthusiasts will draw a direct comparison with the four-cylinder Series 1 Discovery

Above right: The early dash was reasonable for 1970, but looks decidedly dated and austere nowadays. This early four-speeder has no overdrive (which did not arrive until 1978), plenty of instrument blanks and a three-spoke steering wheel, which someone must have thought was a good idea. (Mark Clark)

Right: No shortage of luggage space! It was as Spartan here . . . (Mark Clark)

Mpi which suffered, as would a similarly engined Range Rover, from lack of power, torque and, ultimately, buyers.)

Because David Bache's design department was weighed down with work relating to the V8-engined Rover saloons, the initial styling was prepared by King and Bashford. Later tidied up by Bache's stylists, it was proposed as a two-door car only, despite protests from the sales people who (quite rightly) could see the possibilities, practicalities and extra sales if it had four doors. But safety regulations could be met more easily by a two-door model. For increased safety, the front seat belts were included in the seats themselves, to prevent the possibility of rear-seat passengers tripping over loose belts as they got in and out. It is interesting to note that one of the aspects of the 'tidying' operation was the twin castellations on the bonnet; market research carried out when planning both subsequent models showed it was an essential feature of the Range Rover, to the extent that the 'new' models had to have them, too!

Originally, the idea was to use selectable 4WD like

the Land Rover and front suspension which bore more than a passing resemblance to that of the Ford Bronco. Both of these were found to be unsuitable; the V8's torque was just too much for a single axle, and so permanent 4WD was decided upon, thus splitting the torque two-ways. Although the 'borrowed' suspension layout seemed good on paper, it resulted in massive kick-back through the steering. The first batch of pre-production cars were made with aluminium bonnets, but it was found that they cracked very easily and so production models featured steel bonnets.

. . . as it was for the passengers, where vinyl ruled on the door trim, seats and floor coverings. Just right for hosing down after a day on the farm – but not very likely! (Mark Clark)

The Velar

All companies have to test vehicles on public roads before they are launched and it is considered important that they are disguised in some way. Land Rover cunningly badged all the pre-production models with the name Velar. However, Velar had actually already been used before – on a Rover sports car which only made it as far as the prototype stage. (Incredibly, it has survived and now leads a life of leisure at the Heritage Motor Centre, Gaydon, a Mecca for all enthusiasts of British cars.)

There is some debate over how this name came about; some say it was from the Spanish Velar and others, from the Italian Velare. However, as the car was the brainchild of an Alvis (then part of Rover) engineer,

Land Rover eventually got round to adding doors for the rear seat passengers in 1981, which massively extended its appeal, although they did take some length from the load-bay. You can create a heated discussion to while away those long winter nights by debating whether the practical considerations of the four-door model ruined the essential 'rightness' of the original design. (Nick Dimbleby)

it's no surprise to find that Velar is simply a word created from some letters from each of the companies. Alternatively, it stood for *V*ee *E*ight *LA*nd *R*over. So Velars – around 40 were built – had the name across the bonnet in Range Rover style, although the lettering was cobbled together from the then current P6 Rover model and in true 'Blue Peter' style, the 'A' of the word was actually an upside-down 'V'.

Despite being launched in 1970, the first Velar hit the streets during the summer of love – 1967, and while most of the known universe debated the true meaning of *Sgt Pepper*, those earnest lads at Lode Lane were engaged in more constructive behaviour. The final Velar was made in January 1970 and was, as near as damn it, what would hit the showrooms later that year. Those first cars are, not surprisingly, very much sought after and there is even a special section for them in the Range Rover Register.

Launch of the Range Rover

It is rather ironic that the years described as 'the decade that taste forgot' (i.e. the 1970s) gave birth to one of the finest vehicles ever to come from this

country. One can only assume that its style and, without a doubt, taste, stemmed from the fact that its inception went well back into the 1960s, when Britain seemed to lead the world in, well, just about everything. And let's face it, the decade which gave us the Beatles has got to be good!

The launch of the Range Rover was originally planned to be an impressive bash, even for an industry where truly expensive launches are *de rigueur*. Big budgets were being readied for an exotic on/off road experience in North Africa. In the way that only the British can manage, this became tea and stickies at the Meudon Hotel in Cornwall. Nevertheless, in May and June 1970 those journalists who troubled to make the

Left: The four-spoke steering wheel replaced the rather staid three-spoke item in 1979 for the 1980 model year. Note also the carpets and semi-trimmed seats – signs of things to come. (Nick Dimbleby)

Below: Perhaps the first real inkling of the Range Rover's ultimate aim was the involvement in 1981 with the top fashion magazine, *Vogue*. A special edition was launched (and called the In Vogue) with another one following in 1982 and again in 1983, each time the specification getting more luxurious. The 'In' part of the nomenclature was dropped in 1984, and after then, the Vogue became Range Rover's top model and the one to aspire to. Early models came equipped with niceties like this picnic set.

The Range Rover's front door hinges were rather clumsy items and very much on show, reflecting its Land Rover heritage (it doesn't matter what it looks like if it does the job). The same applied to the large and ugly bonnet hinges which were replaced by hidden hinges in 1986, for the '87 model year . . .

. . . but it was 1989 before the door hinges had the same treatment.

journey to the deep South West were seriously impressed by a vehicle so unique as to create a new marketing niche in the UK.

In truth, there had been nothing like it; previously, permanent 4WD vehicles had been sluggish and agricultural, apparently designed by Lego and offering all the driver enjoyment of a trip to the dentist. But here was a car that accelerated quicker than most family cars and, better still, could cruise at over 90mph. And all this without sacrificing practicalities – the horizontal split-fold tailgate meant that large loads could be heaved into the cavernous luggage area (made bigger still by folding forward the rear seat) and the weight was handled easily because of the Boge Hydromat self-levelling strut. There was enough power and torque from the lusty, 3.5-litre V8 engine to tow the

proverbial three-bed semi and stopping presented no problems for the fully servo'd, four-disc system. As all the floor mats were plain vinyl, it could be hosed out after a hard day on the farm or, as at the launch, a hard day charging around the Blue Hills Mine in St Agnes (a site more used to seeing motorcycle trials competitions).

Sales began on 1 September that year and straightaway, demand outstripped supply, so much so, that many delivery-mileage examples were being sold by profit-motivated owners at a healthy premium over the list price. The official factory tag was £1,998.00 and although early models featured a limited slip differential, it was deleted at the end of the year.

In the first six months, it was awarded the Don Safety Trophy and a Gold Medal for its coachwork. During 1971 it picked up the RAC Dewar award for outstanding technical achievement and became the only vehicle ever to be exhibited at the Louvre museum in Paris, as an example of modern automotive art.

Among the first options on offer from Land Rover were a towbar, laminated windscreen, fog lamps and heated rear screen. On the downside, the projected production figure of 250 cars a week was massively optimistic and by the end of the year, less than half that total had been achieved, despite a queue of eager buyers stretching over the horizon.

It's well-known that the long-awaited four-door Range Rover did not appear until 1981, but it is hard to credit that the initial prototypes were being worked on in 1972. Even more unbelievable is that the eventual design was virtually the same, even down to the parts-bin Morris Marina door handles, that stayed with the car until its demise in 1995. After two years on the scene, the price had risen to £2,134.

The first major revisions occurred in 1973, when brushed-nylon upholstery (the first overt sign that Land Rover realised that the target market wasn't all farmers after all), inertia reel seat belts and power steering became available as options. The rear wash-wipe system was very welcome, as the rear screen got very dirty in the rain and cosmetically, the rear 'D' pillars were covered in black vinyl. The diff-lock warning light was moved from within the console-mounted switch to the dashboard and an electric fuel pump was made standard. Overall, changes were few but of course, the company was going through troubled times and with cash and organisation being equally thin on the ground,

A typical, top-spec Range Rover – or not. Look closely and you will see that as well as the colour-coded bumpers, star-pattern TWR wheels and body kit, there is something not quite 'right' with the dimensions. This is an LSE model, first seen at the end of 1992 and fitted with a 4.2-litre, 200bhp engine, automatic transmission, electronic traction control and electronic air suspension – a world first for 4x4 vehicles. The air suspension, along with its extended wheel base of 108-inch, was of course a tryout for the S2 car, waiting in the wings. (Rimmer Bros)

A far cry from those early dashboards. This very late model dash is awash with gadgets, gizmos and buttons aplenty. Note wood inlays along the doors, dash, gear lever and surround and, well, just about everywhere in an effort to create the luxury Jaguar/Mercedes feel – the Range Rover's new intended market. The restrictions of the original design are still obvious – locating the radio in a cramped and awkward position in the centre was far from ergonomic, but . . .
(Rimmer Bros)

. . . putting remote control buttons on the steering wheel did help and added even more to the upmarket feel of the car. Build quality, though, was still not really up to scratch; the plastics were quite brittle and the fit and finish left something to be desired.
(Rimmer Bros)

it was to be some time before real progress could be made. Despite this, the waiting list for new cars continued to grow, something not lost on the competition.

Year on year, the '70s saw only slight modifications, most reflecting the needs of the buyers, more likely to be filling the back with bottles of Beaujolais than bales of hay. Improved carpeting on the transmission tunnel was seen in 1974 along with twin, roof-mounted interior lights. The first 'option pack' was announced in 1975, which included power steering, tinted glass, brushed-nylon seats, front seat head-rests and front inertia reel seat belts. In 1976, the single tailpipe exhaust was replaced by the more efficient twin pipe set-up and the gearing in the transfer box was raised by five per cent. Improving engine efficiency and raising the gearing was an attempt to enhance fuel economy, a real concern at the time, despite the affluent nature of many purchasers.

The following year, the optional exterior mirrors were moved from the bonnet edges to the doors and the engine compression ratio was reduced from 8.25:1 to 8.13:1. High-mileage users welcomed 1978 because a Fairey overdrive became an option, reducing sound levels at higher speeds and improving mpg on long journeys. Not quite so important was the fact that windscreen wipers were finished in black.

The 1980 model was introduced at the end of the previous year (as is still customary with many car makers) and there were plenty of visible changes. The steel bumpers were replaced by black polyester-coated items whilst the raised bonnet lettering (which allowed water to get behind and start rusting) was changed to more practical but less interesting stick-on badging. In a similar vein, the front wing badges disappeared. The new rear lamp assemblies included foglamps and at the front, quartz headlamps improved forward vision. Previously an option, Sundym tinted glass was standardised as were door mirrors, brushed-nylon seats with PVC headrests and front inertia reel seat belts. The redesign of the dash gave extra ventilation outlets and two more warning lamps (brake vacuum loss and fog lamps) and the plain, three-spoke steering wheel was replaced by a more up-to-date four-spoke item. For the first time, that most upmarket of options, air conditioning, was available. So as not to alienate fleet buyers with a car loaded-up with expensive goodies, the Fleet Line model was introduced, which, not surprisingly, was rather basic in its content. Never

awfully popular with its intended market, the specialist converters did rather like them and used them as the basis for ever more luxurious vehicles.

The new decade saw the first semi-official four-door Range Rover, actually a vehicle produced by the Swiss specialist car maker, Peter Monteverdi. The eponymous conversion, complete with upmarket spec including air conditioning and leather seats, was to be sold through Land Rover dealers. It should have done well, but only around 50 found buyers and ultimately, Land Rover's own four-door model (introduced a year later) put

In 1994, the so-called 'soft dash' arrived, being a more comprehensive redesign with some attention being paid to ergonomics. It also featured a driver airbag and, where specified . . . (Rimmer Bros)

paid to the vehicle. Towards the end of the year, the 1981 models appeared with more anti-corrosion protection for the chassis, better upholstery and more carpeting. The wide gate on the four-speed gearbox was narrowed a little in an attempt to make it more wieldy in everyday use.

In February 1981, the limited edition In Vogue model was announced and showed that the marketing boys had really cottoned on to the possibilities of promoting the car with the top-people's fashion mag. *Vogue* photographers took the special vehicle (which had walnut door cappings, centre console, alloy wheels, stainless steel rear tailgate cappings and air conditioning) on a fashion shoot to Biarritz for new collections from Jaeger and Lancim. It was predictably well-received and throughout the year, the general specifications were raised, with such niceties as a passenger sun visor with light, interior light delay and front seat map pockets. The cars were converted from standard by specialists, Wood & Pickett.

Below: The final Series 1 Range Rover (by then renamed as the Classic) was driven off the production line by TV personality (and serious Range Rover enthusiast) Noel Edmunds on Thursday, 22 February 1996. MD Ian Robertson said: 'This is a day of mixed emotions. It is the first time we have ever ceased production of a Land Rover model. The Classic has spawned such world-beaters as the new Range Rover and the Discovery which have allowed us to break into new markets such as the United States and Japan. It's a case of 'The King is dead – Long live the King'.' All told, 317,615 original Range Rovers were produced.

The Range Rover Classic 25th Anniversary Final Edition was launched in 1995. It was based on the Vogue SE and featured a number plaque on the dashboard – only 25 were made. A 3.9-litre, 181bhp engine provided the 'go' and inside, luxury was the order of the day, with standard leather seats, central locking (linked to a comprehensive alarm system) and radio/cassette with CD autochanger. All 25 cars were finished in Oxford Blue metallic, with chrome bumpers, Freestyle alloy wheels and suitable badging on the front wings. Predictably, this has become one of the classic Classics to look out for.

In the July, the big news was the introduction of the four-door model, something long overdue and eagerly awaited by family buyers (who happily traded a little rear load space, part and parcel of fitting a couple of extra doors).

The themes of previous years were continued in 1982, with a host of minor changes and improvements, such as rubber corners on the bumpers and changing the pointless centre speaker grille to a coin tray. Importantly, the steering column switches had to meet European ISO standards and were changed to have the indicators stalk on the left and the lights on the right. The most important aspect of the year was the introduction – just 12 years late! – of an automatic gearbox. This was very important because the executive car-buyer, the new target market, did not expect to have to shift his own ratios. To celebrate, a second special edition In Vogue model was launched. Featuring the new three-speeder, and although the auto option was most welcome, the ageing Chrysler Torqueflite was hardly state of the art. In use it was rather clunky but it was considerably better than the 'agricultural' four-speed manual unit and filled the gap until a better unit could be adopted. In fact, the original manual box lasted only another year before it was replaced by a more user-friendly five-speed box, a beefed-up version of that used in Rover's cars. Four-door cars had their locks moved to within the handles and quarterlights were deleted altogether, which meant that a larger mirror could be fitted. The Vogue model lost the 'In' and became a regular production model with uprated interior/exterior trim, four-speaker radio/cassette and headlamp washers.

In 1985, came a development which will affect all restorers – the bolt-together Range Rover frame was ditched in favour of a totally welded variant. It was brought about by the need for Land Rover to dramatically improve the panel fitment in order to enter the American market. Clearly, the poor old British would accept lower build quality! It was also the year of fuel

Opposite: Land Rover used the Range Rover as a way of opening up the American market again. This seriously modified S1 would take some stopping! Nice registration number, too. (Nick Dimbleby)

injection, the 3.5-litre V8 at last shedding the carburettors which meant more power and more torque while using less fuel. The first model to be so-equipped was, of course, the Vogue. It also gained a front spoiler, twin driving lamps and protective side rubbing strips. All manual cars now had an improved, five-speed gearbox and the radio/cassette deck was moved to the revised centre console. The rear suspension became better with the introduction of dual-rate springs and twin forward-facing dampers. But by far the most significant development was the introduction of the impressive, four-speed ZF automatic gearbox. Smooth

For many owners, the only solution to the V8's thirst for fuel is to fit a diesel. It seems that almost any engine will fit under the Range Rover's engine bay, and that there's nothing that owners won't try! This is a four-cylinder, 3.5-litre Nissan turbo diesel which sits in the bay as if it were made for it. Some aren't quite as successful. In most diesel conversions, the extra weight of the engine requires some uprating of the suspension and brakes. There are many companies specialising in such conversions and as some are better than others, it is wise to find a previously satisfied customer before parting with your cash. Remember that your insurance company will need to be notified and that there may well be an extra premium or special terms applied.

and reliable, it stayed in service until the end of the line.

For followers of the marque, it must have been like waiting for a bus – within a few short years, the car had been given a five-speed manual 'box, a three-speed then a four-speed automatic gearbox and fuel injection on the V8; all that was needed was the long, long-awaited diesel, which arrived in 1986. The Turbo D model was fitted with the Italian VM 2.4-litre turbocharged indirect injection unit. Land Rover did its best to promote it, but it was rather a disappointment after a 16-year wait.

Towards the end of the year, the '87 changes were applied, the most obvious of which were the horizontally slatted 'plastic' grille which replaced the old vertical metal version, the side repeater indicator lamps were moved down towards the front bumper, and the fuel filler cap was hidden under a flap, thus smoothing out the flanks. Concealing the bonnet hinges brought the exterior appearance more up-to-date as did the fitment of plastic wraparound end caps on the bumpers. At the back of the car, the aerial was incorporated in the rear screen de-misting element and, not before time, the tailgate handle was moved inside the car. The two-door model was discontinued (for the UK market) and all four-door V8 models featured fuel

injection. The LT230R transfer box was replaced by the LT230T. In the cabin, the two-spoke wheel was fitted, extra warning lights were located in the binnacle and the extremely useful 1/3–2/3 split folding rear seat made its first appearance.

During 1987, the roof design was slightly modified, which now had no ribbing over the front seat occupants, and the brake servo was uprated. Under the bonnet, the more efficient, Lucas 'hot-wire' fuel injection system was fitted to V8 engines, but by far the most important aspect of the year was the launch of the Range Rover in North America, with a specification more or less the same as the UK Vogue.

For 1988, Land Rover introduced the Vogue SE (Special Equipment) model as its new 'flagship'; it featured air conditioning, four-speed auto transmission, Connolly hide upholstery and electric tilt/slide sunroof as standard. The Borg-Warner chain-driven transfer box and viscous control unit (VCU) was introduced to replace the noisy, gear-driven type. The VCU locked the central differential automatically the instant that traction was lost, removing the need for separate diff-lock switching.

The driver could also now use wipers with a variable speed delay, clean the headlamps using heated headlamp washer jets, stay cooler, longer thanks to improved heating and ventilation and had no need to lock the tailgate separately, as the central locking had been upgraded to include the top rear tailgate. The door trims were more modern, featuring integral armrests, larger storage bins and flush locking buttons while speakers in the lower door panels were optional. At the front of the car, the front spoiler was changed slightly to include four slots in its lower edge. It was disappointing for UK enthusiasts to find that the bigger, 3.9-litre V8 model was for USA consumption only.

By 1989, the Range Rover was doing lots of business Stateside; the 3.5-litre catalyst-equipped model won the 'Four-wheeler of the year' award and the 3.9-litre Range Rover won the *Motorweek* award USA for best multi-purpose vehicle. Good news for non-Americans was that the 3.5-litre V8 was superseded by the 3.9-litre version. The Vogue now had a catalyst exhaust system as standard and it was optional on other models. Attention was paid to stopping the cars as well as making them go, with all models receiving ventilated front discs and asbestos-free brake pads. The Vogue SE also benefited from Wabco anti-lock brakes as standard – optional on other models. After just 19 years(!), Land Rover made the outmoded door hinges flush with the

bodywork and the Land Rover oval badge was added to the front grille. Keep your eyes peeled for the Vogue SE model, which had six, rather than four slots in the lower edge of its front spoiler. The interior continued its rise upmarket with another revised instrument console featuring an electronic speedometer, multi-point central locking (previously, it could only be operated from the driver's door) and Vogue models had their soundproofing levels increased to match those of the SE. Diesel fans were pleased to see that the VM engine went up in size slightly to 2.5 litres, although it still failed to impress overall, especially given the level of some of the (mainly Japanese) competition.

Land Rover started the new decade with a special edition two-door Range Rover. The CSK used the initials of its originator, Charles Spencer King, and featured a host of 'goodies' including five-spoke alloy wheels (a new option for all models), anti-roll bars, extra driving lamps, chromed bumpers and leather seats/door trim panels. Each model also featured a number plaque in the centre console. Almost all were 3.9-litre V8 powered running through a five-speed gearbox.

All models were fitted with a polyurethane deformable safety fuel tank, which meant moving the filler cap higher in the rear wing. Front and rear anti-roll bars graced the Vogue and Vogue SE models but only the latter received standard cruise control, an electric automatic anti-dazzle mirror and glass sunroof (rather than a solid steel one). Heated door locks became standard and the SE-only six slot spoiler was now fitted to the Vogue and oddly, Turbo D, models.

Left: However, for other owners only too much is enough, and a 3.5-litre V8 is just a starting point. Overfinch has been converting Range Rovers for many years, and with considerable success. Until recently, all have revolved around the 5.7-litre, Chevy engine, coupled with a suitable GM automatic gearbox and ancillaries (brakes, suspension etc) uprated to suit. This is an early carburettor conversion, a 570T launched in 1982. No doubt that hugely understressed engine is still rumbling around somewhere! Only with the S3 cars have they broken with tradition, retaining the original BMW V8 unit – albeit with around 100bhp more to play with.

Below left: Overfinch spent lots of money and time developing the Range Rover's high-speed handling to match the uprated performance. This photo of their test car at speed on the Millbrook test circuit shows the gains available – there's barely a trace of roll, despite the fact that the driver is obviously 'pressing on'.

The following year, all models were fitted with anti-roll bars (said to increase roll stiffness by a startling 25 per cent). The LT77 five-speed manual gearbox was replaced by the uprated LT77S unit. Inside the car, heated front seats became options (standard on the Vogue SE) and leather non-electric seats on the Vogue. Vogue/SE owners could get iced-up with a Clarion radio cassette and six-disc CD autochanger with six-speaker system.

Another limited edition car was introduced in 1992: the Brooklands Green. Towards the end of the year, the long-awaited, long-wheelbase (108in) Vogue LSE appeared. It was an open secret that the longer car would be used as a mobile test rig for the Series 2 Range Rover. The increased weight demanded some extra engine, so the V8 was enlarged again to 4.2 litres (some 200bhp) which drove through an automatic gearbox, electronic traction control and – a world first for 4x4 vehicles – electronic air suspension. Redesigning

The emergency services were quick to see the benefit of a high-powered 4WD machine and the long arm of the law soon reached out and grabbed the Range Rover, realising its many virtues were ideally suited to police work. Now used by all forces, the first to take delivery was the Cheshire Constabulary in 1971. From the start, the Range Rover was an ideal candidate for Police work. It was bigger than an equivalent saloon and so could carry much more equipment, a vital point, especially for the increasingly necessary motorway patrol work. The Range Rover's excellent reputation as a tow car was part of its appeal, removing cars (and sometimes lorries!) quickly and without drama from the hard shoulder. Moreover, it had power and performance enough to reach an accident as quick as most 'normal' patrol cars and of course, it could give chase across the kind of terrain a saloon just could not attempt. (Nick Dimbleby)

Left: The same sort of thing applied to the ambulance services, and last but not least . . . (Nick Dimbleby)

Below left: . . . the fire services. The armed forces used Range Rovers as Rapid Intervention Vehicles, designing them 'in-house' and basing them on a specially extended and modified chassis made by Carmichael. The most obvious difference (among a whole host) was the addition of a couple of extra wheels. There were various bodywork suppliers including Carmichael (as here) and Gloucester Saro. (Nick Dimbleby)

Below: It seems that regardless of how much effort anyone puts into a vehicle design, someone always has a better idea of how it should be done. Forget about the standard, long-wheelbase LSE, check out this extra long-wheelbase special. (Nick Dimbleby)

the luggage area and raising the folding cover meant that suitcases could now be loaded end-on. Extras on the options list included new alloy wheels (the TWR 'star' pattern) and a body styling kit.

Oil-burning enthusiasts were rewarded for their patience when Land Rover's own 200 Tdi unit (turbo-charged direct injection) found a home in the Range Rover (after being available in the Discovery since its

DID YOU KNOW?

In 1972, a British Trans-America Expedition took a convoy of Range Rovers from Alaska to Cape Horn. They were the first cars ever to complete that journey.

launch in 1989). All V8 models had catalyst exhaust systems and the three Vogue models came with ETC (electronic traction control) and ABS anti-lock braking.

In 1994, time was clearly running out for the original Range Rover, which at almost quarter of a century, had lasted two or three times longer than many of its contemporaries. (Indeed, its successor managed just eight years . . .) Production of all two-door models ended in January as a new 'smooth look' dashboard was introduced on four-door models, complete with driver and passenger airbags (the first off-roader to feature them as standard). The Vogue LSE had a body styling kit, 'Cyclone' alloy wheels as standard and side intrusion bars on all four doors ('lesser' models only had them in the front doors). Another safety feature was the addition of extensions to the front bumpers, usually referred to as 'crash cans'. The LT77S five-speed

More down-to-earth is this home-brewed effort, the huge roll cage and mud-splattered paint job indicates that this was made for some serious off-roading. At the rear, it's been 'bob-tailed', i.e. shortened, to remove the overhang and give it Defender 90-style hill-climbing prowess. Wheels are steel Discovery with MT (mud terrain) tyres. Note that the rear windows have been panelled over and the raised fuel filler suggests that the tank is inside the car, again to save it from damage off-road.

Above: Of course, for those who want to mix-and-match Defender and Range Rover, there's no reason not to, as this impressive conversion shows. (Nick Dimbleby)

Below: Of course, once some folk get started with the chainsaw there's just no stopping them – a Range Rover cabrio if you please. (Nick Dimbleby)

The Dakar 4x4 (or 'Super Buggy') is effectively a beach-buggy style vehicle based on the Range Rover chassis, suspension and four-wheel drive system. Any of the Rover V8 engines can be fitted (or you could slot in a 5.7-litre Chevrolet unit as seen earlier). At 1,500kg, it weighs 500kg less than the standard Range Rover, which improves top speed and acceleration. Off-road performance is improved still further thanks to better approach and departure angles. If you're wondering why it looks familiar, yet you have never seen one on the road, that is because it was used by Anneka Rice in the BBC TV programme *Challenge Anneka*. For five series it required nothing other than basic servicing.

gearbox was replaced by the R380 unit, with unaltered ratios.

The diesel models received the uprated 300 Tdi engine and, in recognition of the growing importance of diesels, SE trim and automatic options became available on such diesel variants for the first time. When the 'new' Range Rover was launched in September, the original model continued to be produced and became the 'Classic' so as to differentiate it from the Series 2 car.

The big event of 1995 was the convoy organised by the Range Rover Register; on 29 April, 25 cars – one from each year of production – were driven from Solihull to the Tower of London, with various press and photo calls along the way.

The Range Rover Classic 25th Anniversary Final Edition was launched at the London Motor Show, marking the end of Classic production. Based on the Vogue SE, just 25 were built, each one featuring a numbered plaque on the fascia. The 3.9-litre engine produced 181bhp and 231lb ft of torque. All models were finished in Oxford Blue metallic paintwork, with chrome bumpers and 'Anniversary' badging on the front wings.

The interior was finished in Light Stone Beige with leather seat facings and a high line radio/cassette and CD system was standard. The standard central locking was linked to an alarm system with random electronic code selection. Its price on announcement – a mere £40,000! – was some £38,000 more than its opening price, a quarter of a century earlier. Despite this, sales presented no problem, as eager enthusiasts surged to buy it and even today, it remains highly desirable, not least because of its 'loaded' specification. But it had to happen, and it did – production stopped in 1996; the last Range Rover Classic left the production line on 22 February 1996 after a production life of 26 years and 317,615 cars.

Onwards and upwards – the Series 2

Looking back at the 1990s, the whole decade seemed to be a raft of new car launches. However, the Series 2 Range Rover stands out, first and foremost because it replaced a model that was launched over 25 years previously! Quite startling, really, in an age where a four-year old car is virtually a pensioner. The S2 was officially announced on 29 September 1994 and for a while, the S1 production continued alongside the newcomer – not very often do you see that, either. To avoid confusion, the original car was renamed (and badged) the 'Classic', although future confusion was assured by everyone's insistence on calling the later car the 'new'

Range Rover throughout its life – the obvious problem occurring when the next 'new' Range Rover arrived. Many enthusiasts refer to the car by its Land Rover code number of P38A, so they at least know what's what, but it hardly trips off the tongue. Its original codename within Land Rover was Pegasus, although few people refer to it as such now. In the manner of the original Land Rovers, we shall call it the Series 2.

The same – but different. The new Range Rover carried over the essence of the Series 1 including the trademark bonnet flutes and horizontally split rear tailgate. This is an HSE model.

The car became available in the UK in October and throughout Western Europe (France, Spain, Italy, Germany, Holland, Belgium, Switzerland, Austria, Sweden, Norway and Denmark) and many overseas markets including the Far East and Eastern Europe. It went on sale in the USA, Canada, Australia, the Middle East, Africa and Eastern Europe early in 1995.

The S2 Range Rover was the culmination of a £300 million investment programme and no small amount of market research. This included £70 million spent on new facilities at the Solihull site. The component parts of the Range Rover would come together first in the Body in White (BIW) plant where 130 employees would produce 16 body shells per hour. A total of 260 body panels from Rover Body Pressings at their Swindon plant made up each shell, all being supplied as individual panels with the exception of the bonnet, which arrived as a complete assembly. Over £3 million went on upgrading the existing paint shop, the new facility being one of the largest in the UK and

situated on three floors of a self-contained unit. The first stage in the paint shop was the application of a zinc phosphate conversion, applied in an eight-stage spray process. Corrosion protection was taken further by PVC seam sealing and underbody coating carried out prior to primer surfacer paint application by high-voltage electrostatic equipment. Vulnerable panels had an extra coating of stone chip protection.

It was clearly important to Land Rover as a company that the current crop of Range Rover fans were not alienated by the need to modernise the new car and take it even further upmarket than the final Classic series. Surveys suggested that what the buying public liked were things such as the commanding driving position, distinctive twin-fluted bonnet, large areas of glass and horizontally split tailgate – all of these facets were transferred to a lesser or greater extent to the new car. The marketing department discovered that Range Rover customers were among the most loyal in the world – they repeatedly revisited their dealers to buy a new model rather than switch to an alternative luxury saloon. In addition, a large proportion of customers for the Series 2 would already own a Range Rover.

What lies beneath: a cut-away showing the car was essentially what Land Rover had been doing best for almost 50 years. Despite the mass of electronics, other advanced technology and use of better materials, it was a separate body fixed to a strong and separate chassis.

The S2 was slightly larger all round which gave more headroom, legroom and 50 per cent more luggage space. In smoothing off some of the chiselled edges of the previous model, the Range Rover arrived with a 0.39 drag coefficient – not likely to win awards when compared to many conventional vehicles, but it was the best ever achieved by an off-road vehicle.

BeCM

One of the key features of the S2 was the much-vaunted Body electronic Control Module – soon reduced in the way of all motor manufacturers to a set of initials. The BeCM controlled the interior and exterior electrical functions and communicated with all other major functions of the vehicle. It directly controlled: exterior and interior lighting, seat/door mirror memories, windows and sunroof, security system, instrumentation, wash/wipe features and convenience features.

It constantly 'talked' to all other systems to give advanced level of driver control, passing on its findings through the Message Centre. This was a wholly electronic instrument pack containing two clusters of primary and secondary warning lamps with primary mandatory warnings in red and advisory warnings in amber. It could show a total of 150 warnings/messages

Inside the car, all was opulence. This shot shows that much more thought had been given to ergonomic considerations when compared to the basic layout of the original.

covering every function from automatic gear selection to right heights and speeds, airbag faults, to bulb failures. It could even tell the driver when the battery in the alarm remote transmitter needed replacing!

Initial line-up

At launch, there were five models on offer in the UK, all of which featured four doors (five, if you count it like a hatchback), electric windows, power steering, twin air-bags, electronic air suspension, ABS anti-lock braking, side impact bars, height adjustable seat belts, and remote control alarm system with ultrasonic interior protection and passive immobilisation – check out the rather more Spartan specification of those first cars back in 1970 when 'steering wheel' was just about the sum total! The twin-pocket halogen headlamps were power-ful – so much so, in fact, that even on dipped beam, they emitted twice the European minimum requirement. The car easily met the new angled and offset barrier tests, devised in Germany, and crash cans between the front bumpers and the chassis absorbed the impact of minor

Left: Under the bonnet, the extra complexity was immediately obvious, with great disappointment in store for cat-swingers. This is the 4.6-litre petrol engine (the 4.0-litre is virtually indistinguishable), the absolute last gasp from the factory in terms of boring out the venerable V8 that served the company so well for so long. (Nick Dimbleby)

Below left: The straight-six BMW diesel engine was no less crowded. It was popular for being smooth and frugal, although most agree, a little extra torque wouldn't have gone amiss. Companies such as Jeremy Fearn and van Aaken have produced some interesting and easy-to-fit items to give both power and torque a welcome boost. (Nick Dimbleby)

Right: The rear seat passengers had little to complain about, especially if the owner had specified leather trim, as most did.

Below: The long wheelbase meant that there was no shortage of space in the luggage area and the relocation of the spare wheel in an under-floor well meant that . . .

bumps. This meant that damage to the body or other components would be minimised – along with repair bills. The body was made from a combination of long-lasting zinc-coated galvanised steel and lightweight aluminium alloys. The strong chassis was reworked to provide 'crumple' zones, which would sacrifice themselves in a crash to absorb energy and protect the cabin and its occupants. The 'base' models were the 190bhp 4.0-litre V8 and the 136bhp 2.5DT turbo diesel.

The 4.0SE and 2.5DSE had all the standard stuff plus extras such as a heated front screen, cruise control with speed warning control, five-hole alloy wheels, an uprated RDS radio/cassette-based stereo with eight speakers (the base models had a more modest standard RDS radio/cassette deck, and just six speakers), comprehensive climate control with side-to-side settings, leather seats, heated front seats, bib spoiler and headlamp wash/wipe.

The big daddy of the range, the 225bhp 4.6HSE, came loaded with even more goodies, a long list of which included; traction control (rear wheels only), exterior electric heated mirrors, driver's seat memory, an improved stereo system with top model RDS

Above left: . . . the nearside panel could now be used for the optional CD autochanger.

Above right: Inside, just about everything was electric or electronic – certainly, on the HSE model, it was hard to think of anything the driver had to do for himself, except drive!

Below: The petrol-engined cars were bound by law to be fitted with catalytic exhaust systems. These reduced emissions but were far from cheap to replace – there are now stainless-steel versions on the market, as here. (Rimmer Bros)

Opposite: Die-hard S1 fans tended to regard its usurper as a rich executive's toy or school-run special. This line-up of 4.6 HSE cars, some way off the beaten track, gives the lie to this. (Nick Dimbleby)

Suspension

The electronically controlled air suspension was a further development of that 'tested' on the later S1 models. It automatically adjusted the height of the vehicle to suit different driving and road conditions. For example, if a trailer with a heavy load was being towed, the car would still retain its level poise, meaning that acceleration, braking and handling would be unaffected and at night, the headlamps would still be lighting up the road rather than annoying owls. In addition, the driver could select one of five manual settings for access, low, standard, high or extended. The access height was 65mm below standard and could be selected up to 40 seconds after engine switch-off, or up to 40 seconds before coming to a halt. The low position was 25mm below standard and it could be locked there regardless of speed.

The air suspension, tried out successfully on the last of the Series 1 cars, was fitted to all Series 2 models, with only a few modifications. It worked extremely well, offering lots of choice to the user. However, it can be finicky and requires some specialist, i.e. expensive equipment, to set it up. (Rimmer Bros)

All models across the range were fitted with alloy wheels from the off. This is Land Rover's Mondial style.

radio/cassette deck, CD autochanger, 11 speakers and sub-woofer, tilt and slide glass sunroof with one-touch open/close, leather steering wheel with cruise control and stereo switches, and 255 series tyres wrapped around 8in-wide wheels. All engine options were fitted with catalytic converters and the two 4.0-litre V8 models were available with either a manual or automatic gearbox, whereas there was no auto option for the diesels and no manual option on the HSE. A total of 14 exterior colours were available and the interiors were either Saddle Brown or Granite Grey with cloth or leather seats.

Above: It was to be expected that die-hard S1 fans would regard the new model as a usurper and that, whatever its merits were, it was more boulevard cruiser than hill-hopper. Not so, as we can see here, with this S2 driver making light work of this serious incline and . . . (Nick Dimbleby)

Left: . . . what Range Rover driver is going to let a mere river get in the way? It brings to mind the effective '80s advertising campaign with the strapline 'I brake for fish'. Quite. (Nick Dimbleby)

Below: There is no doubt that the Series 2 Range Rover presented a tasty morsel for the car thief, and so plenty of thought was given to security. An alarm/immobiliser was fitted to all models and visible VIN plates were fitted to the dashboard, as here.

The specially developed all-terrain lightweight articulating suspension system used composite arms to link the rear axle and chassis. This cushioned passengers from bumps while providing accurate cornering and allowing plenty of 'feel' for the driver.

Transmission

All models were, of course, permanent four-wheel drive and featured a viscous coupling unit on the central differential. Quite rightly, much was made of the automatic gearbox 'H-gate', a world-first, developed by Land Rover engineers and one which allowed the driver to select either high or low ratio using just one lever. The H-gate also provided control for both the automatic transmission and transfer box via the same lever, removing the need for a transfer box lever. The selector lever incorporated a two-stage button; the first stage allowed movement through the auto gears and the second allowed the change across the gate from high to low ratio.

High-to-low and low-to-high changes could be made 'on the fly' at speeds of up to 5mph, although the company still recommended that they be made with the vehicle stationary.

Luxury, security – and then some

A definite weak point on the outgoing cars was that of security, something that was addressed with the Series 2. Press the remote control fob to lock the car and it deadlocked the doors, disabled the sill buttons/interior door handles and locked the tailgate. From the outside, it could be used to shut the windows and sunroof. If the 'unlock' button was pressed accidentally, the car would not remain vulnerable for long – if a minute went by without a door being opened, it would automatically re-lock itself. On removing the key from the ignition, the engine was automatically immobilised and a battery back-up meant that the siren would still sound even if a thief cut the power leads. Operating the remote locking key on the HSE model would automatically program the

seat, headrest and door mirror positions to the correct position – the spare key could be used to program a second set of positions for another driver. Another neat HSE feature was that when reverse gear was selected, the electric door mirrors would adjust automatically. And another feature – it had an electronic interior mirror which dimmed and lightened automatically. Predictably, as the age of the cup-holder dawned, the HSE had four.

On SE models, the electronic systems would tell you how far you could travel on the fuel remaining. The cruise control could be set in 1mph increments and the speed warning control could be set to any point between 20mph and 100mph in 5mph increments, sounding an audible alert if the limit was exceeded.

Prices

At the launch, the prices reflected the Range Rover's rise in status and equipment levels, and it is hard not to ponder that in 1970, the original car cost £2 less than £2,000.

4·0 V8	£31,950.00
2·5DT	£31,950.00
4·0 V8 SE	£36,100.00
2·5 DSE	£36,100.00
4·6 HSE	£43,950.00

Autobiography

The Autobiography programme was truly an inspired piece of marketing, building on an already high-end vehicle by taking its equipment levels – and price – into another league altogether. Land Rover had realised with the S1 that the more exclusive the vehicle, the less important the price because there will be someone, somewhere quite happy to pay it. Introduced in 1995, the programme could be applied to the 4.0SE and 4.6HSE derivatives and it enabled the customer some measure of choice over certain areas of the specification. Inside was a virtual forest of burr walnut fascia trim supplied in two options; the Superior included the trim around the instrument binnacle, dashboard console, air conditioning fascia, gearshift

---

DID YOU KNOW?

That early S1 Range Rovers were only ever intended to be fitted with steel wheels and so the studs are not long enough for alloy wheels. Although many owners do retro-fit alloys, it's a potentially dangerous practice. You can check whether your wheel studs are suitable by looking for a triangle stamped in the outer end of each stud – if it's there, you can use suitable alloy wheels with no worries.

Opposite above: When you need a little extra space, just extend the car. Oh, and add another axle while you're about it! (Nick Dimbleby)

Opposite below: Like the S1, a great many Series 2 cars were used as the basis for totally new vehicles – one could hardly call a 3-axle, 6 wheel cabrio with three rows of seats 'modified'! (Nick Dimbleby)

surround, ashtray, gearshift knob, console. The fascia side cheeks were leather clad and the top rail was burr walnut. Those selecting the Deluxe option had all the aforementioned plus a burr walnut switch panel, cubby lid, rear ashtray, rear vent, handbrake lever. In addition, the handbrake gaiter and cubby box were covered with leather. There was Connolly high-grade leather (customer choice of colour, naturally) and the seats could be standard or traditional English style, with or without perforated seat facings.

The prices for the 1996 model year were, as follows, and already shifting inexorably skywards:

4·0 V8	£32,850.00
2·5 DT	£32,850.00
4·0 V8 SE	£37,200.00
2·5 DSE	£37,200.00
4·6 HSE	£44,850.00

Automatically diesel

The big news a year after the car's launch was announced at the Frankfurt Motor Show in September 1995 and it revolved around the two diesel models – an automatic gearbox was to be offered. In addition, the DSE model was fitted with cruise control as standard. The 'box in question was the ZF HP22 four-speed unit, first used on the 4.0-litre V8 cars, not least because it was specifically designed for installation in the Range Rover and was, therefore, ideally suited to handling lots of torque, especially in off-road or towing situations. It was essentially the same, save for a lower first gear ratio. The electronic gearbox incorporated EAT

The 4.0-litre V8 models gave away a little power to the mighty HSE cars, but there was little else to choose until you looked really hard at the standard equipment list – even then, a few well-chosen extras could lift the specification without suffering the thirst of the larger engine.

(electronic adaptive transmission) and Range Rover's unique H-gate, hi-lo gear change. EAT provided a series of shift patterns which adapted automatically to the driving style of the individual – gentle driving accessed one pattern, more 'enthusiastic' driving selected another. In high range, the driver selected either 'normal' or 'sport' mode; in the former, a base gear shift pattern was activated, one tuned for optimum drivability and economy under urban and motorway conditions. Three additional gear shift programmes operated, invisibly to the driver, adjusting to vehicle and engine loading, road/ground conditions and throttle position. In low range, the gearbox behaved as a manual transmission and could be locked in any gear as required. As on the petrol models, the transfer box was a Borg-Warner unit fitted with range selection operated by an electric motor and controlled by a dedicated electronic control unit.

On-the-road prices for the 1997 model year had again sneaked up to:

4·0 V8	£35,130.00
2·5 DT	£35,130.00
4·0 V8 SE	£39,715.00
2·5 DSE	£39,715.00
4·6 HSE	£47,765.00

Above: Initiated in 1995 soon after the launch of the S2, the Autobiography programme was a huge success, enabling those customers with sufficiently deep pockets to pick and choose a specific list of features from the catalogue. This 2001 model seems to have at least one of everything!

Below: There was good news at the end of 1995 for diesel owners, when it was announced that the DT and DSE models were to be offered with the ZF HP22 automatic gearbox as an option.

Satellite navigation is commonplace nowadays, but it was not available as a Land Rover fitment until 1997, when the CARiN Special Edition Range Rover was launched in a limited production run of 30 vehicles.

Luxury stratosphere ahead

In July 1997, Land Rover announced a production run of 100 *really* luxurious Range Rovers named, rather unadventurously, the Limited Edition. It was based on the 4.6-litre HSE and was recognisable from the outside by a list of specific features; British Racing Green metallic paint (a new finish) colour-coded bumpers, sills and door mirrors, a cream coachline and 18in five-spoke Mondial alloy wheels. Inside, the interior was Lightstone leather with contrasting dark green piping on the seats. The price of a little more exclusivity was £53,000 on the road.

At the same time, and to herald the introduction of satellite navigation (satnav) into the Range Rover specification, the CARiN Special Edition Range Rover was launched. (CARiN was the impressive Philips-developed satnav system fitted as standard to many vehicles throughout Europe at the time.) As well as having this most unusual of electronic aids, it also had British Racing Green metallic paint and 18in triple sport alloy wheels, pale parchment leather interior trim with perforated seat facings and contrasting Lincoln Green piping and carpet over rugs. In addition, there was a full walnut deluxe interior taken from the Autobiography programme. The whole package cost a hefty £63,000.00 on the road.

Introduced in June 1998, the Range Rover diesel dHSE featured a host of standard upgrades including, five-spoke alloy wheels, electronic traction control, automatic transmission and eight-speaker ICE system. Of course, with this higher specification came a higher price of £47,075.00.

This was a good year for Land Rover, with 18,000 Range Rovers sold in the first eight months of the year. By way of a celebration, a raft of updates was introduced for the 1998 model year. Six new paint colours were added to the list and there were new alloy wheel styles available for the base and SE models, with all wheels now coming with a 'jewelled' Land Rover badge in the centre caps. All derivatives were fitted with an alloy (rather than steel) spare wheel and a bib spoiler was made standard on the SE and HSE models. To meet EU legislative requirements, a high-mounted, centre rear brake lamp became standard issue and all models except the diesel automatic, came complete with twin front fog lamps as standard.

The cloth seats, standard on base models, were revised with a new seat pattern and the deletion of piping while the leather seating, standard on the SE, DSE and HSE derivatives, was revised in a traditional British six-flute style. All models – regardless of seat material – were fitted with leather-trimmed gear controls. The SE and DSE models featured walnut door cappings. The ICE systems were upgraded, as the popularity of music on the move continued to grow, with the base system being an eight-speaker set-up and the SE and DSE models getting a 10-speaker version. The top-of-the-heap HSE received a rather nice Harman-Kardon system with improved amplifiers and speakers.

The exhaust catalysts were revised on the petrol-engined models and EGR (exhaust gas recirculation) exhausts were fitted to diesel-engined cars. Range Rover watchers were not surprised to see the prices rise once more, the span now being £38,250.00 to £49,326.00.

In June 1998, an upmarket diesel model was announced. That a 'mere' diesel should come so fully loaded reflected a changing market and the increase in importance that diesel engines had taken on over the years. Standard equipment on the Range Rover diesel dHSE model included an eight-speaker ICE system with CD autochanger, Lightstone leather fringe upholstery with electric seats, five-spoke alloy wheels, electronic traction control and automatic transmission. It was available in a selection of metallic paint finishes: Oxford or Cobar Blue, Epsom Green, Rioja Red, Niagara Grey and White Gold. All models had colour-coded bumpers, side sills and door mirrors. All this came at a substantial premium over the standard diesel cars, costing £47,075.00 on the road.

For the 1999 model year, with over 100,000 Series 2 cars already sold, the Range Rover line-up offered improved specification across the board. The V8 engine was substantially revised, as detailed in 'Thor hammers home a point' below. The traction control system was modified and extended to all four wheels, offering improved grip in gripless situations, such as driving in ice or snow. The system adjusted automatically for road conditions (both on and off-road) ensuring that forward motion was maintained even if individual wheels lost grip. All models were fitted with four airbags as standard, viz. full-sized driver and passenger airbags and a thorax system integrated into both front seats providing protection for both front seat occupants in the event of a side or offset impact. Seat belt pre-tensioners with load limiters were also standard across the range. Two new body colour options were added with Blenheim Silver replacing Altai Silver and Beluga Black making way for Java. With such luxurious vehicles, wheels (alloy, naturally) and tyres were an important part of the package and were available as follows:

Model	Wheel type	Wheel size	Tyre size
4.0 V8 & 2.5 DT	Typhoon	16 x 8	225 x 16
4.0 V8 SE & 2.5 DSE	Spyder	16 x 8	225 x 16
4.6 HSE	Lightning	16 x 8	225 x 16
All model options	Mondial	18 x 18	225 x 18
	Hurricane	18 x 18	225 x 18

Prices with effect from 1 November 1998 were:

4·0 V8 Automatic	£40,995.00
2·5DT	£36,640.00
4·0 V8 SE Automatic	£44,035.00
2·5 DSE	£42,700.00
4·6 HSE	£51,165.00

A glance down the then current option list revealed how much extra you could add to your chosen vehicle:

Automatic transmission	£1,530.00
Electric (non-memory) seats	£1,075.00
Electric sunroof	£1,075.00
Premium ICE (over mid-line)	£1,075.00
18in alloy wheels	£1,970.00
Hurricane 18in alloy wheels	£1,970.00
Lightning 18in alloy wheels	£885.00
Heated seats/windscreen	£540.00

Thor hammers home a point

In 1998 (the 1999 model year), the latest development of the all-alloy V8 engine was ready. Developed under the codename Thor, it spearheaded the attack made by

the Series 2 Discovery but at the same time, was slotted under the bonnet of the Range Rover. Even the casual observer couldn't help but spot the different unit, distinctive as it was with the new 'bunch of bananas' inlet manifold. Tuned to increase torque, it had twin plenum chambers and long curved induction tracts, exploiting resonance effects for more effective cylinder filling. It is also considerably more compact than the previous 'penthouse' intake plenum, giving better underbonnet access – and doesn't it just look good?

The engine was blessed with the Bosch Motronic 5.2.1 engine management system, similar to that used on the BMW 7 and 8 Series models. This provided high precision control of the sequential fuel injection and distributorless ignition, with full provision to meet worldwide environmental legislation, including the latest American OBD (on-board diagnostics) requirements. An important aspect of this new ignition package was the adoption of special long-life double platinum (or 'platinum rivet') spark plugs, capable of running, maintenance-free for an incredible 72,000 miles. Two twin-ignition coils (that's four coils in all) fed two cylinders simultaneously providing the direct ignition according to the ECM programme.

New silicon HT leads with high-temperature resistance and increased durability were specified. Another new aspect of the engine, and something tried out first on the Freelander, was the returnless fuel rail, with pressure regulation being carried out by a pressure relief valve within the submerged high-pressure fuel pump in the fuel tank. This simplified the fuel system, with the benefit of increased reliability and reduced

maintenance. The revised layout for the heater and engine coolant system (including a diesel Td5-like bottom-hose-mounted thermostat) necessitated modified rocker covers. As on the Td5 diesel, there were four colour-coded poly-vee belts to suit the various permutations of the ancillary serpentine drive. (The Td5 unit was used on the 'new' Discovery, launched in 1998.)

In May 1999, a new diesel model was launched, building on the success of the diesel HSE of the previous year. The dHSE was powered by the 2.5-litre BMW engine as usual, with the differences being the vehicle's specification. Standard on all models were: full leather interior, climate control, four-wheel traction control, anti-lock brakes, front and side airbags, 11-speaker ICE system with steering wheel controls, electronic memory driver's seat and door mirror positioning.

At the British International Motor Show of October 2000, Land Rover announced a new Range Rover line-up designed '. . . to enhance its appeal as one of Europe's top luxury cars'. It was to be available in three distinct derivatives, namely: County, HSE and Vogue, together with three limited edition models: Range Rover 30th Anniversary, Holland & Holland, and the Linley. All this, of course, was in addition to the Autobiography programme. By this time, the prices for the 'standard' vehicles were £40,000 for the County, £46,000 for the HSE and a heady £53,000 for the Vogue.

The County had leather seats, Mirage 16in alloy wheels and was available with either a 4.0-litre petrol or 2.5-litre diesel engine. If required, a manual gearbox was a no-cost option only on the diesel-engined car. The HSE model was unchanged from its previous high-specification which included electric front seats (memory on driver's side), automatic adjustment of external mirrors, climate control, Harman-Kardon 11-speaker ICE system and burr walnut door cappings and fascia trim.

DID YOU KNOW?

That the aluminium roof of the S1 models simply screws into place. So, if you have a sunroof problem, or if the roof is damaged, you just replace the whole lot – easy!

At the top of the range, the Vogue had lots to offer, starting with a Philips' CARiN II satellite navigation CARiN II satnav and including a wood/leather steering wheel, burr walnut on the centre console and an electronic driver information system. A wide variety of colours and trim options was available including Oxford leather and colour-keyed carpets. The ICE system featured 12 speakers with digital sound processing.

Happy 30th birthday

The 30th Anniversary model made its debut at the Geneva Motor Show in March of 2000 and was, obviously, produced to celebrate 30 years of Range Rover production. Using elements from the Autobiography programme, only 500 were produced, each having a unique '30th Anniversary' badge. The cars were finished in Wimbledon Green (the bumpers, mirror heads and sills were colour-coded) and fitted with 18in Hurricane wheels. Inside, Classic Green leather seats with Lightstone piping complemented the exterior finish. The leather detailing was also on the doors, steering wheel, handbrake grip and auto change gear lever. Burr maple wood veneer was applied to the console, gear surround, fascia and

door rails. CARiN II satnav meant that clumsy road atlases could be confined to the bin – as could arguments with the front seat passenger! Only 50 vehicles were fitted with an option pack which consisted of additional veneer on the instruments, wood veneer on the folding picnic tables and a DVD player complete with twin screens fitted into the front seat headrests. Customers paid £57,500 for the 'basic' model and an extra £6,000 for the option-pack.

Holland & Holland

Holland & Holland is a world-renowned manufacturer of sporting guns and clothing. The special model was finished in Tintern Green and rolled on 18in Hurricane wheels with Tintern Green inserts. The interior was made to look and feel like your average country saddlery with dark brown bridle leather and oil walnut

Making its debut at the Geneva Motor Show in March of 2000 was the 30th Anniversary special edition, of which 500 were produced to celebrate 30 years of Range Rover production. All were colour-coded in Wimbledon Green with 18in Hurricane wheels and with lots of special features; £57,500 bought you the 'basic' model, with the DVD option pack an extra £6,000.

Above: Again in 2001, yet another special edition – you'd never guess that there was a new model on the horizon: 200 Bordeaux cars were made, all were automatics and based on either the 4.0-litre V8 or the diesel engine.

Below: In its last year of production, there were few outward changes to the S2 Range Rover, but the most obvious as seen here, being the twin circular headlamps.

The line of evolution showing at front, the first Range Rover to leave the factory (although this was actually chassis No. 3), a long-wheelbase Series 1 'Classic' in the centre, and at top, a Series 2.

'gunstock' wood trim and engraved steel inlays. The exterior and interior chrome work was rendered in blue/black shadow finish. For those who actually wanted to use the car in the country, walnut brown over-rugs were fitted along with brown rubber floor mats. Included were picnic tables in matching gunstock veneer and in the rear of the car was a complete set of Holland & Holland luggage. The price when new was £64,495, plus an extra £5,000 if you specified the optional TV/video system.

Linley

The Linley model (referring to designer David Linley) was described by Land Rover as 'the most exclusive Range Rover of all' – perhaps they should have added 'so far'! It had Linley's Metropolitan range of furniture to which end the car was finished in Black solid paint-work with shadowchrome 18in wheels. The interior had black leather throughout – including the headlining on

the parcel shelf. The full wood veneer had a piano black finish, relieved by stainless etching in a starburst graphic. The general treatment also extended to the picnic tables and centre console surround to the satnav and TV/video systems. With a price tag of £100,000 it was unsurprisingly, available to special order only.

Westminster

Another truly British name for this special edition, again first shown at the Geneva Motor Show. Just 400 were produced, based on the existing Vogue model and supplied in Bonatti Grey, a colour new for the 2001 model year. The bumpers, mirrors and spoiler were colour-coded, shadowchrome 18in Hurricane alloy wheels were fitted and a 'Westminster' badge was applied to the rear tailgate.

Bordeaux

On 28 June 2001, the Range Rover Bordeaux was announced, ostensibly to celebrate 30 years of Range Rover production (although not to be confused with the Range Rover 30th Anniversary model). It had claret coloured paintwork (actually Alveston Red), with matching bumpers/sills and the 18in Pro-Sport alloy wheels featured Alveston Red detailing. The Bordeaux, of which 200 were made (all automatics, 100 4.0-litre petrol and 100 2.5-litre diesel), also featured Light Stone leather seating, with claret red piping and matching carpets. On-the-road price to discerning owners was £38,995.

Final Series 2 Range Rover

The last S2 Range Rover rolled off the production line on 13 December 2001 after a production run of seven years and a total of 167,259 vehicles produced. The Alveston Red, North American-specification

It didn't take the aftermarket boys long to get cracking with some trick bits for the S2. Wheels, tyres, spoilers, colour-coding and an LPG conversion make this one a bit special. (Nick Dimbleby)

model was driven off the line by John Hall, chief programme engineer for the project and Spen King, the man behind the original Range Rover concept. The keys were then presented by manufacturing manager, Mark Footman, to Julie Tew, managing director of the Heritage Motor Centre in Warwickshire, where the vehicle is now displayed alongside other significant Land Rovers, including the first production Land Rover from 1948 and the last Classic Range Rover produced in 1996. Land Rover's director of manufacturing, Martin Burela, commented: 'The second-generation model set new benchmarks in the industry and has proven a continual success throughout its seven-year life.'

And so, the King is dead – long live the King.

The world's most capable vehicle – the Series 3

'We believe the new Range Rover is the world's most capable vehicle, with the greatest breadth of ability of any vehicle ever made. This mixture of peerless off-road ability combined with on-road excellence should satisfy the most demanding luxury car buyer.' Words from Land Rover's President, Bob Dover, which suggested that there was no lack of confidence in the new car.

The Series 3 Range Rover was conceived when Land Rover was owned by BMW, but delivered by the new Ford-appointed management, led by Bob Dover. Dr Reitzle left BMW to join the Ford Motor Company in April 1999, becoming President of Ford's Premier Automotive Group (PAG). He was instrumental in the

purchase of Land Rover from BMW in July 2000 when the company joined Jaguar, Aston Martin, Volvo and Lincoln as part of PAG. Dr Reitzle said: 'Land Rover is the world's pre-eminent manufacturer of four-wheel-drive vehicles and the Range Rover is the original luxury SUV. The new Range Rover is truly extraordinary. Its unique combination of go-anywhere skill and luxury means its closest rivals aren't other 4x4s, but the finest luxury saloons in the world.' The good doctor is hardly

Below: A stunning backdrop; a stunning car. (Nick Dimbleby)

Right: Fancy a paddle? A mere river won't stop the Range Rover. (Nick Dimbleby)

Land Rover's press department arranged heavy snow for the launch in Scotland. The sort of weather that makes you think of a huge log fire – or a Range Rover. (Nick Dimbleby)

unbiased, and has a certain axe to grind, but on paper specification alone, it is hard to argue, and when you get in the driving seat . . .

And just who does get to sit behind that luxury leather wheel? According to Land Rover itself, the typical S3 buyer would have one, or more likely, two other cars to choose from and a joint income of 'around £90,000 a year'. Given the thirst of that big V8 as it lugs around all that weight, this would seem to be a conservative salary estimate . . .

Launch

The Series 3 Range Rover was launched officially in a welter of media hype and spectacle to 200 hand-picked guests at the Design Museum in London. The unveiling was carried out by Bob Dover, while also present were Land Rover's design director Geoff Upex and Dr

Wolfgang Reitzle. Volume production of the car started on 3 December 2001 at Land Rover's Solihull manufacturing plant (in facilities representing an investment of £200 million). The original 'for sale' date was 15 February 2002, although this was a little ambitious and was soon put back a month to 15 March. Anyone miffed about having to wait an extra month could relax in the knowledge that all Series 3 Range Rovers would be covered by a three-year, unlimited mileage warranty. This was introduced as standard on all Land Rover products on 1 March (previously, there had been a 60,000-mile restriction). In addition, there was a six-year anti-perforation warranty and comprehensive, three-years' roadside assistance coverage in the UK and Europe. Within a year (by 1 March 2003) Land Rover went a step further in encouraging buyers by launching the VIP five-year maintenance programme. It covered the costs of servicing and replacement parts for five years, worth around £3,000, for a cost of just £500.

On-the-road prices at launch were:

TD6 SE	£42,995.00
V8 SE	£49,995.00
TD6 HSE	£45,995.00
V8 HSE	£52,995.00
TD6 Vogue	£51,995.00
V8 Vogue	£59,995.00

Testing

But the launch was the tip of the iceberg, as project L322 (the factory codename) was a long time coming. In fact, world testing started three years beforehand, in a 25-country programme which included North and South America, Middle and Far East, Africa and Australasia. Extreme conditions were the order of the day from thrashing around the Nürburgring race track to tackling the Tokyo rush hour. It covered over 9,000 high-speed miles towing a 3.5-tonne trailer in northern Greece. (The Range Rover handled this with ease, but such was the fierce pace of the test that the trailer had to be rebuilt at the end of each day!) Testing in England was hardly glam-

The Series 3 underwent a staggering 1.5 million miles of testing, being put into all sorts of extreme conditions, including going to play in the sand – of the Sahara Desert and . . .

orous and given the usual weather conditions, perhaps it was suitable that Eastnor Castle saw the cars being driven for 250 non-stop miles through thick, sticky mud. The vehicle's wading abilities were tested in the Blair Atholl estate in Scotland and a quarry in southern England was used to check water ingress – or rather, lack of it.

DID YOU KNOW?

That despite massive demand, which outstretched supply for many years, a diesel-engined Range Rover was not available from the factory for 16 years – the first official car being produced in 1986 and was fitted with the unloved, 2.4-litre VM engine.

... the dry, dusty heights of Mexico. Note the headlamps taped-off to prevent 'scoop' shots and rivals getting design details before Land Rover was ready.

Exterior

As with the previous model, the company took care to keep those Range Rover trademarks – the practical horizontally split tailgate, the bold upright front with its simple grille, the commanding driving position, the 'floating' roof, the clamshell bonnet with its castellations and the almost rectangular interplay between the horizontal and vertical body lines. Although a much smoother vehicle all round than the original, 1970 model, the styling cues are still clearly visible.

To add some 21st century elements, the headlamps and tail lamps have a look of their own and down the back of the front wings are distinctive and functional power vents (classic car buffs may well make comparisons with the Chevrolet Corvette). One of the most distinctive exterior features is the headlamp arrangement – they are actually Bi-Xenon units – providing high intensity 'blue' light on both dipped and main beam and, as a by-product, a stylish and instantly recognisable face, an essential marketing point.

At the rear, virtually instant-on LED brake lights give following motorists early warning that the car is slowing. PDC (park distance control) should ease the minds of those worried about bashing a bumper – sensors set in the bumper measure the distance to an object, giving an audible warning to the driver. Another very useful electronic option is the tyre pressure monitoring system; sensors in the tyres keep an eye on

the pressures, alerting the driver if there is an appreciable difference. (For aftermarket versions of both these products, see Chapter Eight.)

Engines

As with the Series 2, there is a choice of petrol or diesel power plants. Both the units offer better performance, lower emissions, improved fuel economy and greater refinement over their predecessors. Both are BMW-sourced, but have been modified to suit their now very different life under the Range Rover bonnet. In each case, the air intake is repositioned to permit deep wading and changes were made to the sump to protect against water ingress. Changes were also made to the seals and tougher front bearings on timing pulleys were adapted. New oil systems with revised oilways and ventilation have been developed to enable the engines to deliver while the car is on a 45° gradient or traversing ground with a side angle of 35°.

Both engines have dual throttle maps and more electronic trickery whereby the car reacts differently depending on circumstances. When driving on a normal road surface, the throttle has a fairly quick response, as usual, but during off-road driving, where a quick

The Series 3 Range Rover is an imposing vehicle, and no mistake. Lots of styling cues from the previous two models were retained and the bi-xenon headlamps gave it an instantly recognisable 'face', an essential marketing tool in an era where cars all seem to have been made from the same mould.

The rear is no less impressive and again, the lamps make it look different to most of the opposition (although there's a real Freelander look about them). The horizontally split rear tailgate was retained and the lower one is just as practical – it can take the weight of two adults.

Dig deep and you will find lots to look at in the powerful 4.4-litre BMW engine. What a pity . . .

. . . that soundproofing considerations have made it rather dull to look at in situ.

throttle action is definitely not a good thing, the accelerator requires comparatively more pressure for any given rise in engine speed. Clever stuff.

On both engines the exhaust is an impressively hefty, single-piece design. Ever mindful of extreme conditions, they have been designed to cope with ambient temperatures of 50°C.

Petrol

Unlike the Series 2, there is no choice of capacity of petrol V8, although having to make do with the BMW-sourced, 4.4-litre (4,398cc), is no hardship; the 32-valve engine has aluminium alloy cylinder heads and block with four chain-driven cams. Variable camshaft control improves efficiency and response. Power is 282bhp and there is a rather useful 325lb ft of torque. So, despite being of smaller capacity than the 4.6-litre Rover engine, both power and torque are up – by 25 per cent and 10 per cent respectively. The unit meets or exceeds both EU3 and North American LEV emission regulations.

Diesel

The six-cylinder, common rail, turbo diesel engine had been codenamed the Td6 and followed two other Land Rover 'TD' diesels; the Td4, four-cylinder, as featured in the Freelander, and the Td5, as seen in the

S2 Discovery and later Defenders. Compared with the 2.5-litre BMW unit used in the previous generation Range Rovers, it is some 30 per cent more powerful. More importantly, the torque has gone up from 199lb ft to 288lb ft, happily produced at just 2,000rpm – barely more than tickover.

The capacity is a nominal 3 litres (actually 2,926cc), the engine being a cast-iron block on which sits an aluminium cylinder head. Spinning round inside are a pair of chain-driven cams and 24 valves. The turbo has a variable nozzle to give better torque at low engine speeds and improves pick-up when the accelerator is pressed. It complies with EU3 emissions regulations with EGR (exhaust gas recirculation) and CO_2 emissions of 299g/km.

Transmission

Permanent four-wheel drive is, of course, standard as are state-of-the-art, five-speed fully electronic automatic transmissions in petrol and diesel versions. The petrol cars continue a long-standing association with the German ZF company, while the diesel-engined cars come with a GM-sourced unit. These provide both fully automated and Steptronic manual shifts – the best of both worlds from a single 'box – and there is a two-speed transfer gearbox offering a low range for off-road

use and a high range for normal driving. The 'dual mode' feature offers standard or economy mode at the flick of a switch.

A new torque-sensing centre differential continuously and automatically changes the torque bias between front and rear axles depending on available traction, up to a maximum ratio of 2:1 between the axles. A refinement for the new model means that it is now possible to shift from high to low ranges (and vice versa) on the move (high-to-low up to 10mph, low-to-high up to 30mph).

Suspension

Large, tubular sub-frames are used for mounting the suspension and driveline components. The independent suspension is conventional, being MacPherson struts at the front and a double unequal length wishbone set-up with telescopic dampers at the rear. The true enthusiasts who were (understand-ably) worried that the move from an old-fashioned ladder chassis/separate body would mean trouble off-road, needn't have concerned themselves. The S3 actually has *improved* axle articulation – which is something to behold given that its predecessors weren't exactly lacking in this department – and 2.6in more ground clearance.

Introduced late in the lifespan of the Range Rover Classic and featured as standard on the second-generation model, the electronic air suspension (EAS)

Look, Ma – no chassis! This image shows more than any other how the Series 3 has changed from previous incarnations; the monocoque shell replaces the old chassis/separate body arrangement used for over 30 years.

system has been greatly refined and now features interconnected cross-link valves for all four wheels, allowing a stiffer spring rate for road use and a softer spring rate when the vehicle is being driven off-road. Working automatically, the cross-link valves are closed when the vehicle is being driven on metalled roads. In this mode, each wheel acts independently of the other. The obvious benefit here is that the suspension is stiffer and restricts body roll. EAS employs 'terrain sensing' software to determine if the vehicle is off-road at which point it automatically opens the two cross-link valves – the input comes from signals from travel sensors in all four wheels.

The all-singing electronics which control the air suspension, can do the old trick of lowering and raising the vehicle at the flick of a switch while a neat new feature is 'Access'. With this, the driver can pre-set a suitable height to which the vehicle will automatically lower itself at journey's end. Of course, it is automatically self-levelling, thus compensating for heavy loads and counteracting the 'nose in the air' stance that can affect lesser vehicles.

The running gear also features a number of electronic traction control systems including dynamic stability control (DSC – developed in association with Bosch), which takes electronic information from the wheel sensors and operates the ABS braking system in conjunction with the engine, to prevent wheel spin or locking, thus giving maximum control. DSC also knows when the car is towing a trailer and allows for its extra weight in its calculations.

The Series 3 also has the Land Rover-pioneered hill descent control (HDC), first seen on the Freelander. Unlike simple engine braking, HDC provides brake bias to the downhill axles (which depends whether the vehicle is going up or downhill) and can also brake individual wheels as necessary. It can be selected in low or high range and in any gear. The speed of descent

With no chassis on which to fit the underpinnings, there's a separate sub-frame at the front and rear. This is the front showing the large protective tubular 'cradle' for the lower engine and other exposed components, and . . .

. . . this is the rear with a conventional double unequal-length wishbone set-up with telescopic dampers.

depends on the gear selected – the lower the gear, the lower the speed. The standard anti-lock brakes (ABS) are supplemented by emergency brake assist (EBA) and electronic brakeforce distribution (EBD). It's fair to say you actually need a large vehicle to carry all those abbreviations! EBA recognises the need for emergency braking by sensing rapid application of the brakes by the driver. It assists by boosting hydraulic pressure, ensuring maximum retardation efforts under ABS control to maintain vehicle stability and steering feel. EBD automatically compensates for the forward weight transference by equalising braking pressures front and rear. Shields made from Kevlar and plastic are fitted to provide protection for under-car bits and pieces, notably the suspension, lower engine, fuel tank etc.

Interior

In keeping with its luxury role, the vehicle's interior was completely redesigned. Three decorative finishes – traditional burr walnut, Avant-garde Cherry and Sporting Foundry – mixed with seven seat colours, four lower trim colours and two upper trim shades to allow customers to choose a bespoke interior, even before we get to the Autobiography options. Other features include two different leather treatments and chrome dashboard detailing.

Standard and optional equipment levels have been greatly widened to provide new levels of comfort and customer choice. Features available include an integrated telecommunications package such as telephone system with cordless in-car handset, satellite navigation with off-road functionality, and an in-dash widescreen TV.

The world obsession with cup holders continues apace and no fewer than four are provided; better yet, they have been designed to handle just about any cup size there is, from the tall and thin Japanese tea cans to American oversized cups. You'll sleep at night knowing this.

The front seats are luxurious and even more so are the contoured seats which have memory facility, foldable armrests and electronic control of the adjustable backrests and headrests. All seats can be specified with heating elements and so, amazingly, can the steering wheel, which is electronically adjustable and which automatically raises when the ignition key is withdrawn, to aid access to and from the vehicle.

Left: The dash layout came in for universal praise. It's just so ergonomic, so stylish and so, well, good. Leather and wood abound, as befits its status as a luxury vehicle to rival those from BMW, Jaguar and Mercedes. Note the central liquid crystal screen which displays vehicle functions and can also show TV and satnav information (standard on all models).

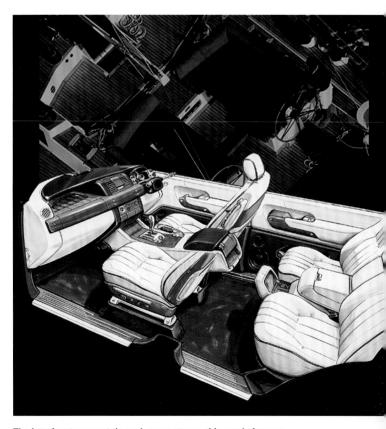

The interior, too, went through many stages, this one being very similar to the final chosen layout and with just a few small changes . . .

. . . this design is virtually what went into the metal.

And the passengers hardly suffer on the journey, either – there are houses that offer less comfort than this.

The heating and ventilation system has dual zone settings for driver and front passenger with rear passengers having their own control. It also compensates for solar heating load and it monitors pollution, switching automatically to recirculated air if exterior pollution levels are too high. For cold climates, climate heating control operates on an independent fuel burning heater, either pre-programmed or using a remote control, so that the car starts with a warm engine and warm interior (see also the Eberspächer heater in Chapter Eight).

All models are equipped with an electric glass sunroof which can be opened in a number of positions. At the rear, a conventional 60/40 split rear seat offered the most versatility and the cargo area has fitted luggage loops for restraining light/small loads. Gaining space inside meant that the car had to get bigger; overall, the new model is 237mm longer, bumper-to-bumper, than its predecessor with a wheelbase some 135mm longer. It is taller, too, by some 45mm. Although the body itself is 67mm wider, the overall width – including the door mirrors – is actually slightly reduced by 37mm. This means more interior room for passengers without making it too unwieldy when driving in heavy traffic. The passengers in question can cart more luggage, as the area available has risen from 513 litres to 535 litres.

In-car entertainment

Three levels of ICE are offered with six or 11 speakers, or 11 speakers with a DSP (digital signal processing) amplifier on the top level. A six-disc CD player is mounted in the passenger glovebox, allowing discs to be changed easily and from within the cabin. Speed-sensitive volume control is standard across the range.

Safety

One of the key areas of safety is that of crumple zones; by definition, a car with long front/rear overhangs will achieve this more easily because there's literally more car to crumple (thus protecting the cabin and its occupants). To get the same results in the Range Rover as most luxury cars was impressive, as the overhangs are deliberately short so as not to hinder off-road performance. Inside, six airbags are fitted – front, side, thorax and head – to protect the front seat passengers and the front side airbags are fitted in the door rather than the seat, as was common at the time. Head protection bags for the rear seat passengers were optional. Each passenger door has side impact protection and all seat belts – including the centre rear – are three-point inertia reel, the front belts having pre-tensioners. Isofix standard fixing points are fitted for the safe fitting of child seats.

Security

The insurers gave the new car their highest rating; the alarm/immobiliser was Thatcham Category 1-approved and includes a siren with battery back-up, volumetric

interior sensing and vehicle tilt sensor. In addition, all models have Superlocking (which deadlocks the doors) and shielded locks. The VIN (vehicle identification number) is marked on important components through the vehicle as well as being visible through the windscreen, thus making falsification very difficult indeed. The large glovebox is lockable and secure, even if the valet key is being used on the car. The centre console has a double lid which provides extra stowage while also improving security.

Autobiography

If Land Rover had been slow off the mark to exploit the sales possibilities of the Series 1 Range Rover, they have certainly learned their corporate lesson by the time the Series 2 arrived. The Autobiography personalisation programme had been extremely popular and, let it be said, profitable. As such, just three months into the Series 3's production life, Autobiography was on the go again. Quite suitably, the launch was held at London's prestigious Canary Wharf.

Two vehicles were on show, packed to the gills with unique veneers, hand-finished leather seats and a mobile theatre system. One was finished in Spectral Red, a Chromaflare paint which gives the appearance of a different hue depending on the viewing angle. Quite how much of a problem it is to touch-up the odd scratch doesn't bear thinking about. The programme includes a raft of options, such as a palette of 25 special colours, (with two Chromaflare shades), a colour-keyed body kit

Below left: Despite all that luxury, the Range Rover remains a totally practical proposition for ferrying five people, lots of luggage and a darn big trailer just about anywhere in the world. (Nick Dimbleby)

and 10 new interior leather trim colourways. Perforated leather seat panels are available and the leather trim includes the lower dash, glove box lid and centre console sides. Four new wood veneers are also available to complement the interior.

The in-car entertainment is taken to a new level in line with the ever-increasing in-car technology and move towards multimedia. Equipment available includes the TV/DVD system which features twin 8.5in screens built into the back of the front seats. The system includes a six-disc auto changer and is fully versatile in that one rear seat passenger can be watching a TV programme while the other enjoys a movie. The 'Logic 7' sound system was developed specially for the Autobiography programme by the Harman-Kardon company and features 14 speakers and a sub-woofer specially tuned to the acoustic

DID YOU KNOW?

That the first four-door Range Rovers weren't actually produced by Land Rover, rather the Swiss firm of Monteverdi in 1980. Only around 50 were sold and production stopped as Land Rover started making its own four-door models for the '81 model year.

Above: When you can't see the wood for the trees, drive over them! The Series 3 shows its mettle here and reveals, to most people's amazement, even more axle articulation than before. (Nick Dimbleby)

Below: Land Rover's G4 Challenge was an attempt to revive the spirit of the defunct Camel Trophy. Various Land Rover vehicles were specially equipped for the rigours of the event, all the same colour as this S3. (Nick Dimbleby)

characteristics of the new vehicle. The TV/DVD and 'Logic 7' sound systems can be combined to form an in-car mobile theatre.

Vehicle security, which is already impressive, can be enhanced as part of an Autobiography package; Land Rover Supaglass is a high-technology coating offering protection against attempted break-ins and prevents broken glass falling into the passenger compartment.

Proof of the pudding . . .

The motoring press was lavish with its praise and sales of the new model were high. In February 2002, it was awarded the 'Car of the Year 2002' by BBC's *Top Gear*. The award was presented by *Top Gear* magazine editor Kevin Blick, who said that the Range Rover was 'luxurious, versatile and imposing' and praised its world-class interior, peerless refinement and excellent driving characteristics. He concluded that 'It's not just

a 4x4 – the Range Rover makes a case for itself as the ultimate Grand Tourer.'

In July 2002, *Auto Express* magazine voted it the 'Best 4x4 off-roader' in the New Car Honours, asserting that 'the no compromises off-roader has just arrived. The Range Rover combines on-road sophistication with peerless off-road ability that defines the word refinement. Where its contemporaries pack their interiors with phoney wood and ruched leather in an effort to generate a luxury feel, the Range Rover does it without breaking sweat.'

In February 2003, less than a year after its launch, the Series 3 Range Rover picked up the Coachmakers Award to Industry. The award was made by the Worshipful Company of Coachmakers and Coach Harness Makers, established in 1677 and one of the oldest trade bodies in the world. The Series 3 was recognised for its 'outstanding contributions to technological advancement in transport and for its elegance and commercial significance.'

Receiving the award, Land Rover's managing director Bob Dover said: 'This is a very prestigious award, as the

Left: Such a superbly integrated design wasn't scribbled on the back of a fag packet! Bringing the car into the 21st century while keeping all those traditional Range Rover traits was an unenviable task, and all manner of designs were tried out . . .

Below: . . . from the sublime to the eye-watering.

Almost there with this one.

names of the previous winners on the trophy suggest –
from Sir William Lyons to Rolls-Royce. Owners, dealers
and the company's employees all over the world should
be very proud of this excellent achievement.' It was
presented by Victor Gauntlett, the former chairman of
Aston Martin Lagonda.

First year sales

It was another record production year for Land Rover in
2002 with LR sales overall topping 47,000 vehicles. The
Series 3 Range Rover had sold more than 5,000 units
since its launch in March. For comparison, the Defender
range came in at around 5,500 sales, the Discovery
11,000 and the Freelander an impressive 24,000 (this
making it the UK's best-selling 4x4).

Sporting times

Predicting the future in motoring terms isn't for the
faint-hearted, but sources suggest that by the end of
2004, there will be a 'baby' Range Rover on sale,
allegedly to be called the Range Rover Sport. It is slated

as being a three or five-door car aimed at the trendy SUV
market and slotting 'twixt the Range Rover and
Discovery, although it will be based on the upcoming
Series 3 Discovery underpinnings. It is reasonable to
expect a Ford engine under the bonnet (see later) but the
diesel option will probably be the TD6, six-cylinder unit.

Engine options

With so many major manufacturers now coming under
the Ford banner, the choice of power plants is wide.
Initially, one might expect Ford to supply an American
V8 or two – after all, few companies have more eight-
cylinder experience. But let's remember that Jaguar now
comes under the sign of the blue oval and the Coventry
company also has plenty to offer, including V6, V8 and
supercharged engines. One extremely intriguing
possibility is that the Range Rover could at some point
be fitted with the Aston Martin V12 power plant. The
queue starts here, folks . . .

Chapter **Five**

Let's off-road!

Despite its rather swish, upmarket image, the Range Rover is a supremely competent off-road machine. If you're cynical, just remember that the basic chassis, suspension and drivetrain layout was hi-jacked for use on the Discovery, the Defender 110 and the off-road enthusiasts' favourite, the Defender 90.

Off-road driving is a whole load of fun and, compared with most other forms of motor 'sport' is extremely safe. As has often been said, it's a great adrenaline rush at just 2mph! But the technique of driving without tarmac under the wheels is absolutely nothing like normal driving and to a great extent, you have to undo much of what you have learned and take on board some weird and wonderful new techniques. You are heartily recommended to try at least one day at a specialist training course, where you can learn the new skills required to be safe off-road. More importantly, perhaps, this will give you an insight into bad-condition driving-control required for driving in snow etc.

You can go off-roading with Land Rover itself, at one of its four sites or with one of the many other off-road centres. Some of these photos were taken at one of David Mitchell's Landcraft off-road days, set in the staggering scenery of Snowdonia National Park and offering terrain of just about every hue. Like many such centres, you can choose between specific training sessions or just turn up and enjoy yourself on the vast acreage of safe off-road tracks. My thanks to David and eager, muddy demonstrators, Paul Delves and Andrew Nay.

Where to go off-roading

Despite the government's best efforts (aided and abetted by many pressure groups, some with rather dubious motives), there are still plenty of green lanes suitable for legal off-roading. However, it is vital that you check and *double-check* that the lanes you use are specified for your use – it is irresponsible to give ammunition to the we-want-the-countryside-for-ourselves brigade. You'll need the very latest, large scale Ordnance Survey maps but even they need checking-up on as changes made to lanes can take some years to appear in print.

From the mud, through the water, up the rocks, between the trees – why do things the easy way? No reason at all when you're wheeling a Range Rover.

Above: Watch out for low-flying buzzards! Climbing up to dizzying heights is all in a day's work for Land Rover's finest and apart from the thrill of achievement, there are other rewards because . . .

Below: . . . even with the morning, mountain mist, it's one heck of a breath-taking view. Being able to carry five people down high-speed motorways and then up to the top here – in the same vehicle! – just emphasises what a great car the Range Rover is.

Off course, you can't let all that practice go to waste – here's a well-equipped Series 1 tackling the notoriously tough Croisière Blanche event, which takes place every year high in the French Alps. A true test of car and driver. (Nick Dimbleby)

By far the best way to approach the subject is to join a local club – either a general 4x4 club or one specifically for Range Rovers and/or Land Rovers. Most have officers who deal with green-laning issues and stay in touch with the local councils to keep tabs on which lanes are officially open to vehicles and which aren't. It also gives you the opportunity to take part in an organised drive which not only adds a pleasant social element to the day, but also means that there's someone to help out should you get it all wrong.

And how would you like to have an interesting day's green-laning, meet lots of like-minded folk and do something for the environment? Well, with the cost of scrapping old vehicles being down to the owner, more and more old wrecks are being dumped in our green and pleasant land. Many clubs are making a point of clearing lanes not only of rotten old cars (dangerous in themselves of course) but also of many years of neglect in terms of waist-high undergrowth, fallen trees and household rubbish. This clearly benefits everyone who wants to use the lane and is one in the eye for certain factions who want to have sole access to such lanes – which have been available to large, wheeled vehicles for many hundreds of years – but who seem to be curiously missing when such maintenance work is required . . .

Preparation

The Range Rover is more or less ready to go, with tyres being probably the most important factor requiring attention. For standard green-laning or a reasonable off-road course, you won't need to do anything much to your car. However, remember that extras such as side steps and a towing bracket will limit your ground clearance and of course the front spoiler (with its lights) is also directly in the firing line. You will need relevant maps, of course; the club experts will tell you which ones. Portable satnav is a boon, especially if you intend to drive off-road then do a little hiking or biking.

It's the driver that needs the most preparation and it's advisable to take at least some off-road training before you venture out solo. Remember that green lanes are public roads and that you and your passengers should wear seat belts at all times. Even on a private site, this is an essential safety measure – imagine up-ending your Range Rover without your seat belts on!

It is definitely not recommended to go off-roading alone for obvious safety reasons. Always take a first-aid kit with you and a 12V tyre-inflator is useful, as it means you can lower the tyre pressures when required, knowing they can be returned to the original figures

Left: Andrew shows how water should be tackled – enter slowly then push forward to create a bow-wave to push the water away from the car. This is more important in deeper water, where it could swamp the engine bay or worse, get back into the exhaust causing the engine to 'hydraulic' – i.e. seize expensively!

Right: This hand-held Magellan Sportrak unit will work equally well in-car, where it shows street-level mapping, as on a day's off-roading or even when you go off for a hike in the middle of nowhere. As you can see from the raindrops, it's wise to get one that's waterproof!

Below: Quagmire is a word that leaps to mind – you wouldn't want the bucket and sponge after this day out! You can see why a set of MT (deep-treaded) tyres are handy for days like this. Check out Paul's grinning offspring enjoying the fun in the back – it beats sitting glued to the Gameboy and is a great way to introduce the next generation of drivers to the delights of off-roading and some great countryside. Don't forget those seat belts, though.

when driving home. CB radio or two-way walkie-talkies are handy tools to have. Carry something in the way of sustenance (a thermos with a hot drink, sandwiches, chocolate etc.) and always make sure you have a full tank of fuel before you start – remember that off-roading can reduce your typical mpg by 50 per cent or even more. Empty the car of non-essential contents and tie everything down that's likely to fly around as the car goes over very uneven surfaces and up steep inclines.

When you come back on to metalled roads, be aware that lots of mud and grit in the wheels, steering and brakes will do them no good at all. Make sure they work efficiently and take the first opportunity you can

Right: A decent set of seat covers is a wise move for off-roading (or even for winter use in rural areas). These are Walser Pro Fit Dirty Harry covers, which are made from tough, waterproof material and have a pocket at the front. They fold up into the pocket for easy storage when not in use and at around £25 a pair, are good value.

Below: Here's proof, if such were needed, that the Series 2 is still up to the mark in off-roading terms. However, I'm glad it's not my car that's dropping off that precipitous piece of rock. (Nick Dimbleby)

to blast them clean. It's a good reason to buy a pressure washer, because no garage forecourt will want you using theirs and clogging up the drains with half a tonne of mud!

Clearance

Make sure you understand and know exactly what your vehicle is capable of. Regardless of your school maths results, there are three angles you need to know, as follows. The approach angle is that between your car and an incline. You need to make sure that your front wheels touch the hill before your front spoiler.

The ramp angle defines the side steepness of a hill – you don't want to get your Range Rover beached on its belly. The departure angle is the opposite of the approach angle and relates to the angle of the hill in relation to the lower rear of the vehicle. The Range Rover isn't bad in this area, although a towing bracket seriously inhibits its performance. And of course, the Series 2 and Series 3 models, are longer overall and thus lose out on some of the versatility of the Classic models. Get any of these wrong and you could damage the vehicle as well as putting yourself (and your passengers) in danger.

Tyres

All the traction in the world is useless if you have no grip, and that's the job of the tyres. Most Range Rovers leave the factory with road-biased tyres fitted, which are usually described as being an 80/20 balance in favour of metalled roads. They'll offer almost saloon car levels of comfort, grip and quiet and be quite capable when dealing with minor off-road excursions. At the other extreme, there's the 'MT' (mud-terrain) type of tyre, which has tread deep enough to swallow small children whole and which will grip in mud and snow like no road tyre. These are designed to clear away the mud as if it wasn't there, and although they can be used on metalled roads, they will compromise cornering and handling and cabin noise levels will increase dramatically.

In common with many enthusiasts, the author lives in a part of the country where bad winter weather is a foregone conclusion – namely above the snow line in the Cambrian mountains. The answer here was to buy a set of cheap, Discovery steel wheels and use them as 'slaves' for a set of serious MT rubber for use from November to March. At that point, the standard alloys can be replaced along with the 'road' tyres. Clearly, this is also a principle that applies if you intend going to off-road days or courses – it takes half an hour or less to change them, so it's hardly hard work. It's advisable to

There is a huge difference between proper off-road tyres and mainly motorway rubber. On the left is a Goodyear MT (mud-terrain) Wrangler, with some cavernous depth tread. The Goodyear Eagle GT+4 on the right, however, has been constructed with tarmac in mind and offers extra on-road cornering and braking, better mileage and improved mpg.

have a decent torque wrench to hand if this is the route you choose – you really don't want to have three wheels on *your* wagon!

Make sure, however, that you only use road-legal tyres if you're going off road down official green lanes. First, these lanes are still classed as public highways, so you would be running illegally otherwise, and secondly, they would churn up the ground in no uncertain fashion, which is something nobody wants.

Gearing down

All Range Rovers have low-range gearing as well as conventional road-biased ratios – known by most as a low box. The gearing is reduced by a ratio of 2:1, and it is this that makes the Range Rover so useful off-road, allowing the car to travel very slowly without the need to use the clutch or brakes and is ideal for coming down steep, muddy hills where using either would result in a

very unpleasant scene indeed. Later models, with ABS traction control *et al*, score highly here, but there's no room for complacency and in many respects, a little tuition on how they should be used is more important than ever.

Land Rover's tread lightly policy

Land Rover itself recommends a policy of TREAD lightly, where the word is a mnemonic listing the essential points of safe and considerate off-roading, viz.

T = Travel only where permitted

Travel only on trails, roads, or land areas that are open to vehicles or other forms of travel. Make sure the trail you plan to use is available for your type of vehicle. Wide vehicles on narrow trails can damage both the trail and your vehicle. Cutting switchbacks or taking short-cuts can destroy vegetation and cause others to use the unauthorised route. Most trails and routes designated for 4x4 use are constructed to withstand the effects of use. Staying on these trails reduces the impacts from 4x4 vehicles.

R = Respect the rights of others

Respect and be courteous to other users who also want to enjoy the lands you are using for your travels. Be considerate and honour their desire for solitude and a peaceful countryside experience. Loud motors and noisy behaviour are not acceptable and detract from a quiet outdoor setting. Give other people the space and quiet you would appreciate. Driving near or around someone's camp site is not appreciated. When driving, be especially cautious around horses or hikers – pull off to the side of the track, shut off your engine, and let them pass.

In and around campgrounds, be sensitive to campers' need for a peaceful atmosphere.

E = Educate yourself

Educate yourself by stopping in and talking with land managers at their office. Or, if you see them in the field, stop and ask questions. They can tell you what areas and routes are suitable for off-roading. Travel maps are usually available at most offices. On private lands, be sure to obtain the owner or land manager's permission to cross or use their lands. As you travel the countryside, comply with trail and road signs. Honour all gates, fences and barriers that are there to protect the natural resources, wildlife and livestock.

A = Avoid streams, meadows and wildlife

Avoid sensitive areas at all times. In early spring and autumn, rains and snow typically saturate the ground making soil surfaces soft. Improper vehicle use can cause damage to vegetation and ground surface. Stay on designated roadways and trails so that new scars are not established. Especially sensitive areas susceptible to scarring are stream banks, lakeshores and meadows. Cross streams only at fords where the road or trail intersects the stream. Travelling in a stream channel is unacceptable and causes damage to aquatic life. Hillside climbing may be a challenge, but once vehicle scars are established, other vehicles follow the same ruts and do long lasting damage. Rains cause further damage by washing deep gullies in tyre ruts. Permanent and unsightly scars result. While operating your 4x4, be sensitive to the life-sustaining needs of wildlife and livestock. In deep snow, stay clear of game, so that vehicle noise and close proximity does not add stress to animals struggling to survive.

D = Drive and travel responsibly

Drive and travel responsibly to protect the forests, lands and waters that you enjoy. You enjoy the outdoors for a number of good reasons: the countryside is beautiful; you have freedom to roam vast scenic areas; you see clear flowing streams and rivers; you see wild game and birds; you breathe clean air; you see and smell fragrant and colourful vegetation, trees, flowers and brush; you develop a sense of being a part of this great and expansive outdoors! These and others are reasons enough for you to do all you can to help protect the lands that mean so much to you.

Help preserve the beauty and the inspiring attributes of our lands for yourself and new generations to follow.

This chapter can only cover the basic rules of driving off-road. For further information, consult *The Off-Road 4-Wheel-Drive Book* by Jack Jackson (Haynes Publishing).

Chapter **Six**

Choosing and buying a Range Rover

My thanks go to Barry Chantler of Dakar Cars, Chris Crane and Holly Hollingsworth of RPi Engineering and Graham Rimmer, Bill Rimmer and Piers Philo of Rimmer Bros for their assistance with the preparation of this chapter.

Buying a Range Rover should be your first step on the off-road to heaven, but for many buyers, it has been the flat-tyre on the highway to hell. Get it right, and you will find that the bug, once it has bitten, will just not let go.

The club connection
So, you're convinced that the Range Rover is for you? The first thing to realise is that Range Rovers (Series 3 excluded) are hardly thin on the ground, so there's no shortage of choice and no reason to rush out and buy a

bad one. As with most cars, membership of the owners club is a good starting place, and in this case, the only specific club in the UK is the Range Rover Register. Here, you will find a repository of information and often, club members who are selling their own cars – and by definition, these tend to be better looked-after than most. It is also a place to meet owners of like mind, and to buy used parts and accessories. See Appendix D for details.

Land Rover's franchised dealership network tends to deal mainly with fairly young Range Rovers. You will pay more here, but as a rule, you will be getting a well-maintained, low-mileage vehicle, with the benefit of a comprehensive warranty. However, for those with smaller wallets, a whole raft of specialist dealers has sprung up to fill a gap in the market.

Pre-buying checks

It is advisable to check the provenance of any car you intend to buy with one of the following agencies – before you hand over any money. Some Land Rover magazines run their own schemes, and it doesn't really matter which you choose to use, as long as you do. Some buyers may try to pressure a sale but remember, there's plenty of good Range Rovers around and if you lose this one, there'll be another one along soon. According to the AA's records, every 12 seconds they come across a vehicle that needs further investigation. A call to one of the organisations listed here will reveal such things as its presence on the stolen vehicle register, whether there is finance owing, a confirmation of the chassis and engine numbers, the vehicle colour, in which country it was originally registered or if it has been written off at some point. The (current) cost of around £35 is nothing compared to the possible loss of many thousands of pounds.

HPI Equifax
01722 413434
www.hpicheck.com

AA Used Car Data Check
0870 600 0838
www.theaa.com

RAC
0870 533 3660
www.rac.co.uk

Look before you leap

Lots of people just jump in and drive off when buying a car, but there is lots to do before you even turn the engine over. Start with a visual check; from across the street the Range Rover should look good, sitting four-square with no obvious leaning and with no nasty oil or coolant puddles beneath it. Its image of being a cut above the rest seems to have transferred itself into the metal and a good Range Rover will always look rather superior to lesser vehicles. If it doesn't, perhaps there's been some uncaring owners.

As you walk round the car, look hard at the paintwork for evidence of respraying (such as 'orange peel' effect, dull patches, slight colour mismatches etc). Kneeling and looking right along the flanks of the car will get you some odd glances, but it will also reveal even the slightest imperfections. Don't be too harsh here, because the aluminium panels are easily damaged and

Range Rovers suffer more than most from the attentions of carelessly opened doors from adjacent vehicles. Remember that wet paintwork on any car will look good. If it's been washed recently or it's just rained, take along a chamois to wipe it clear and show up any possible paintwork flaws. In essence, if it looks down-at-heel and neglected, then it probably is; many drivers buy them, believing they can run them on a Ford Fiesta budget – and they can't.

Paperwork

If you're happy it looks right, then it's on to the paperwork – note this is still before you drive the car. If the V5 (log book) isn't present, come back when it is. It's a common con-trick for it to be mislaid, machine-washed, eaten by the dog etc. Check the number of owners, that the description matches the vehicle (colour, number of doors etc.), the exact age and that the chassis and engine numbers tally. Remember that the VIN number can tell you exactly what the vehicle should be and by cross-referencing with the information given in Appendix C, you will be able to do a quick double-check. Does the VIN plate show signs of tampering? Be suspicious, because Range Rovers are notoriously easy to ring – i.e. give a false identity. The interchangability of the various component parts, not only between other Range Rovers, but between Defenders and Discoverys makes life easy for the thief.

Mileage

Buying a low-mileage car seems to be the Holy Grail for many would-be owners, but there's two sides to every coin. A great many Range Rovers are very low mileage indeed, mostly because the majority are V8-powered and few can cope with the fuel thirst. The downside is that, by definition, the engine must spend much of its time below full working temperature and getting extra fuel from the choke/extra injector, which tends to wash the protective oil from the bores. In addition, low mileage can mean that the car goes many years between services, which is a very bad thing – for example, V8 engine oil needs changing at least once a year regardless of mileage, but an owner doing less than 2,000 miles a year, might well wait a full three years before doing so.

A high-mileage car can often be a much better proposition – and I speak from experience. My own 1990, 3.9 V8 auto, was owned for 10 years by a company director. It was serviced regularly and

In an effort to reduce the number of Range Rovers being stolen, Land Rover introduced a visible VIN system. The VIN (vehicle identification number) was stamped onto the dash as here and was visible through the windscreen. Check this tallies with the V5 along with all the other information.

expensively and had recently been fitted with a new rear tailgate and exhaust. Averaging over 15,000 miles a year, means that it spent much of its time on the motorway, with everything running nice and warm. It sailed through an MoT two weeks after purchase at auction and took its LPG conversion without batting a metaphorical eyelid. Without wanting to tempt providence, it swishes along like the proverbial Swiss watch requiring only the usual maintenance stuff from yours truly – replacement brake pads etc. There's no doubt that a well-maintained Rangie will easily drive through the 200,000-mile barrier. And of course, higher mileages mean lower prices.

Conversions

Many Series 1 Range Rovers have had engine conversions; occasionally, the original VM diesel will have been junked in favour of an alternative, but for the most part, it involves removing the original V8 petrol engine and slotting a diesel engine in its place. These cars need approaching with caution. The best conversion is that which uses Land Rover's own engine and kit of parts (engine mountings etc.). It's more popular (because it's cheaper) to use a Japanese engine of some description, some of which work better than others. The obvious exception to the rule involves a V8-for-V8 swap from those clever folks at Overfinch; until recently, the new engine was a small-block (like 5.7 litres small!) Chevrolet engine offering sufficient power and torque to tow a small stately home along. Invariably, gears were self-selected via a GM auto gearbox. Both items are bullet-proof and spares are readily available – the engine is actually the most prodigious unit in the world, ever! – but approach with plenty of care, as all that 'go' means that it is likely to have been given more right-foot than most. Uprated brakes and suspension should have been part of the original conversion and need checking out with more care than usual as replacements are likely to be expensive. There are other specialists, such as RPi Engineering, that do some smashing uprates and V8 conversions (they always use the original Rover unit as the base) but not all companies can be trusted in the same way.

LPG (liquefied petroleum gas) conversions are becoming increasingly popular, especially with the Series 2 cars. The quality of installation varies alarmingly as there few hard and fast rules and hardly any legislation. An expert is a must when looking at an LPG converted petrol car. Think about where the LPG tank is sited and whether or not it will affect how you want to use it; if it is in the luggage area, it will limit the loads you can take, and if under the front floors, it will limit the car's use off-road. The size of the tank(s) is important, especially if you live in an area where LPG is in limited supply. Remember, that for safety reasons LPG tanks can only be filled to 80 per cent of their total capacity. If anyone tells you they have had theirs changed to take 100 per cent, do *not* get involved, as it makes the entire system extremely dangerous and volatile!

With a conversion of any description, check the attitude of your insurers before you buy. Some companies reach for the barge pole at the mere mention of the word 'conversion' but with alterations becoming more common, it is not the problem it once was. There are plenty of specialist Land Rover insurers around and they understand the nature of the beast. All are likely to want at the very least an engineer's report as to the quality of installation, safety aspects and whether or not the brakes and suspension should be uprated as a result of the change. A typical example is where the relatively light-weight all-alloy V8 is swapped for a cast-iron diesel and the front suspension and brakes should be beefed up accordingly.

General tips

* See the car at the buyer's house – anyone trying to sell a stolen car or a 'ringer' (a car with a false identity) will usually prefer to meet you somewhere else, or come to your house.
* Many crafty thieves park outside someone else's house and just 'happen to be outside with the car' (washing it, maybe) when you arrive, so you assume that the house is theirs. Always try to get inside the house if you can – asking to go to the loo is fair. If the seller hasn't got the house keys ('my daughter has them and has just gone to the supermarket' etc.) then be extremely wary.
* A keen owner will know where all the controls are – an 'owner' fumbling around for basics is a warning sign.
* The more paperwork, the better, especially MoT certificates, which are essential in plotting a car's true mileage.

The buyer's tool kit

* Torch, which lights up awkward nooks and crannies and makes you look like a serious buyer.
* Chamois leather, to wipe away a recent rinse or rain shower.
* Mat or carpet, to kneel on when looking underneath.
* Magnet, to check that what should be steel isn't rust or filler.
* Note pad, with list of salient questions and points.
* Your own detailed list of what the standard specification should be.
* Assistant, preferably knowledgeable, who will also distract the seller so you can concentrate on thorough checking.
* Clipboard and notepad, to keep track of your thoughts – it will also make you look clued-up.
* A good idea of typical prices in your area – they vary across the country.

When to buy

Plan your ownership carefully; study what there is and what you want. Ideally, buy your car in the summer months, for five main reasons:

1. There's lots more light and it means you can view with some confidence in the evenings.
2. It is (or should be . . .) warmer, so you'll be more likely to take your time and thus spot potential problem areas.
3. It is (or should be . . .) dryer and thus you'll be more

inclined to grovel around on the floor looking for underbody damage, oil leaks, rust and rot, worn bushes etc.
4. Psychologically, people buy cabrios and sports cars in the summer and anything with 4WD in the winter. It follows that the prices of any 4WD vehicle will be more during the winter months and less in the summer – which is the time to buy your Range Rover.
5. If the worst happens and you do buy a car that requires work, it's less hardship sorting it out when you're not knee-deep in snow and fighting a −7° wind chill factor.

Range Rover buying checklist

This checklist should be used as a basic guide in conjunction with the more detailed sections in this chapter.

Location, location, location

Try to view at owners' home. Meeting in car parks etc., is suspicious – the car may be stolen. Check its regular parking place for signs of oil/coolant leaks.

Is the log book (V5) present?

STOP NOW! Do *not* buy a Range Rover of any hue without seeing the V5 (see next comment). Don't accept that it was swallowed by the dog or eaten by the washing machine.

Check the V5 details

Make sure everything checks out – name/address, number of owners, engine, chassis and VIN numbers etc. Any discrepancies should be ironed out before continuing. Use the 'numbers' appendix to make sure it is the correct model and has not been doctored in some way.

Is there at least some service history, invoices etc?

Some invoices quote a mileage, so check to see if it makes sense. Older cars probably won't be dealer-serviced but enthusiasts tend to keep every single invoice for parts replaced and service items bought; the less there is, the more you should worry.

Are there any previous MoT certificates?

Again, enthusiasts hoard these and if present, give some idea of the true mileage. Ensure that the mileages tally. An apparently enthusiast-owned Range Rover with no previous MoTs should strike a discord – proceed with caution.

Viewing

Wet, wet, wet

Is it raining or has it rained recently? Has the car just been washed? Bear this in mind – water makes any car's paintwork look better than it is. Take a chamois to wipe the surface clean so you can see what lies beneath.

Are you viewing in fading light?

You really can't inspect a car properly in the dark or half-light. OK, you can get a general impression of a car as dusk falls, but don't buy before you have had a thorough, daylight inspection.

Look hard all around the car

Check along its flanks for accident damage. Look inside the boot and engine bay for minor bumps – check for signs of overspray etc.

Look in the engine bay

Check that the oil and coolant levels are correct – if they're not, it points to inconsistent maintenance and a slap-happy owner. Dirty oil or brown coolant are worrying signs as are oil leaks and a generally scruffy bay.

Look under the car

Check for oil leaks from engine, transmission or dampers – learn the difference between a gentle weep and an expensive drip. Look under wheel arches and along sills for damage or rust. Check exhaust condition.

Wheels and tyres

Check wheels for serious damage – expect minor scuffs. Check tyres for legal tread, uneven patterns, sidewall damage etc.

Look at brake discs and pads through wheels

Damaged and/or scored discs and badly worn pads

mean no test drive until replaced. You should know the cost of replacements.

Interior trim

Check condition is commiserate with mileage. Look for signs of abuse. Remember Range Rover trim was never the best, even when new.

Interior functions

Make sure *everything* electrical works, especially expensive kit such as air conditioning.

Driving

Start the car

It should start easily and idle cleanly straight away – if not, there could be fuel-injection or electronic problems. Give carburettor'd cars a little leeway, as position of choke is important. Push it in as soon as possible to prevent it revving too hard when cold.

Drive the car if possible on a selection of road surfaces

Check all gears engage and stay there. Listen for untoward noises from engine/suspension.

Braking

Brakes should stop the car quickly and in a straight line. Check ABS light operation (where fitted) – incorrect function is an MoT failure point.

After the test drive

Let engine idle for a few minutes then blip the throttle – a puff of blue smoke indicates engine wear, and lots of expense.

Check the provenance

Use HPI, AA, RAC or any company offering similar facilities. The current cost of around £35 could save you many thousands. This essential phone call can reveal if the car has been stolen, written-off, still has finance against it etc., even against a changed 'personal' numberplate.

The deal

Like an auction, set your budget beforehand and stick to it. Know replacement prices and use them as a lever to get to your price. Offset against any spares included in the deal.

The choice

The car you buy has to be the right one for you at the right price. Never forget that there are thousands of Range Rovers for sale now. If you're not totally sure, walk away and find another.

Insurance

Shop around, is the obvious advice. Check out the adverts in the specialist magazines – at the time of writing there were four dealing solely with Land Rover's products. You can cut your costs by opting for a limited-mileage policy, especially as most used Range Rovers tend to be used as second cars. If you're intending to off-road your car, check the policy small print as some will exclude it. Remember also that when driving on an official green-lane, you are technically still on a public highway, so your insurance must be valid. Make sure you're specific about what your car has fitted so there can be no squabbling in the event of a prang. This applies to obvious things such as engine conversions, but also to less obvious items such as bull bars.

Paying the price

The various buying guides will give you a good starting point as to what is a good price and what isn't, although prices will vary depending on the area you're in. Buying from a Land Rover dealer means you pay a premium, but you should get a comprehensive warranty to ease the financial pain. However, the franchises only handle younger/low-mileage cars, and you're unlikely to find all but the very best/most rare Series 1 Range Rovers there now. A raft of 'specialist' dealers has sprung up to cope with those cars that fall through the net. There are some very good ones around, but equally, there's plenty of cowboys ready to lasso the unwary. Take your time, check around and look for personal recommendations if you can. Buying privately is a cheaper way still to acquire a car, but of course, you have no warranty and, as long as the car wasn't falsely described, no comeback at all. Knowing your onions will prevent the tears or alternatively, take someone with you to inspect the car.

This applies even more so to the very cheapest way to buy – at an auction. Buying at a general sale is OK, but limits your options. Probably the best choice is a specialist 4x4 auction, such as those at Brightwells in Leominster. It is of course the buying method with the most risk, but the savings are enormous and usually mean that you will have a large cash safety net to soak up any possible problems. Inspection time is limited

and you are unlikely to be able to drive the cars, although some will allow the engine to be started. You will need to have your cash or a card ready to pay and have some insurance sorted so you can drive home – unless you trailer it. Warranty is typically just one hour and will cover only major problems – a five-speed gearbox which will only select three gears for example. The two major rules are simple: know your stuff or take someone with you who does, and set a price limit before the auction starts *and stick to it!*

And finally . . .

Buy a good Range Rover and you will find yourself hooked on what is arguably Land Rover's best car – although there's many an hour's pub discussion in that sentence! Nevertheless, if you have *any* doubts that you're *not* buying a good one, then the advice is simple and unequivocal: turn on your heel and walk away – hundreds of thousands were made, and there are far too many good ones to waste your time and money on a troublesome car.

Series 1

By far the easiest Range Rover model to buy is the Series 1. There is a lot of choice in all directions: three or five-door, diesel or petrol V8, LPG gas conversions, manual or automatic and all, for the most part, cheaper than the cheapest boring Euro-hatch. And don't forget that if you're prepared to drive a *really* old car (like pre-1972), you get a free gift from the government in the form of no road tax – not very often you can say that, now is it?

Which model?

Until 1986, the engine choice was simple – V8, or V8! It was fed by twin carburettors until 1985 when the relatively simple EFi fuel injection system was introduced (although it took a while for it to become standard across the range). These engines gave more power and torque and were suitably more refined. It is generally agreed that the cars from the late 1980s/early '90s are the best. The 3.9-litre fuel-injected V8 engine is usually thought to give the best blend of power, torque and smooth delivery, although the 4.2-litre offers the most power/torque overall.

If you can't stand its thirst (and don't want an LPG conversion), then there are diesel options. The unloved Italian VM engine was fitted in two capacities from 1986–92 but has a poor reputation and offers lowly power and torque outputs. It was replaced by Land

Rover's own 200 Tdi engine which proved to be much better and this in turn was replaced by the updated 300 Tdi unit in 1994. *Some V8-to-diesel conversions are OK, notably those using official Land Rover parts, but some are absolute abortions; approach with caution, and talk to your insurers before you buy, as they quite naturally, are wary of anything non-standard.*

The four-speed manual gearbox was fitted to all models until 1983. It is undoubtedly as tough as old boots, but betrays its agricultural origins far too readily for such an upmarket vehicle, and high-speed cruising without the Fairey overdrive isn't very kind on the ears or the fuel consumption. Its successor was a five-speed unit based on one used in many Rover cars. It wasn't as hardy but it was much more user-friendly and in general is preferable. Over the years, the level of standard equipment went from virtually nothing to absolutely everything, so if it's gadgets you want, buy the latest model possible. If you need five doors rather than three, you're looking at 1981 onwards. Although it is actually possible to convert a three-door to five, you would have to be really short of something to do with both your time and your cash.

Sad to say, but Range Rover build quality was never the best in the world. The S1, even up to its demise, was screwed together in a manner highly unfitting for its status and price. Exterior panel fit was always a bit hit and miss as was much of the interior trim, which tended to squeak and rattle even when new. This is

Where aluminium outer meets steel inner there's electrolytic reaction which ultimately means corrosion. This is a typical example at the lower front door. All cars will suffer this way, so it is a balance of the extent of the damage against the price and desirability of the car.

another reason to take an expert with you – someone who will understand what is typical of the car in question and what poses something more of a problem.

Bodywork

Almost all the Range Rover outer bodywork is aluminium (Birmabright). It can't rust, but moisture does cause it to corrode over time, bubbling the paintwork and leaving a white powdery finish. It is a soft material and is prone to marking easily. A Rangie without the odd car parking 'ding' is probably one that hasn't left the showroom. But if there's lots of damage, it might mean the car has been driven carelessly or heavily off-roaded. If the latter, it will have taken its toll in other areas, notably underneath. Remember that beneath the aluminium is steel and where the two metals meet, electrolytic reaction occurs, which leads to corrosion and this can be particularly evident on the door skins/frames.

The doors should all open and shut with a solid clunk and not drop slightly as they're opened. Sorting worn hinges/pins is expensive and time-consuming. On five-door models, it is not uncommon to find the rear doors seizing in their hinges, particularly where the car has been owned by someone without a family – a great many Range Rovers are run during their early years as company cars for higher-paid executives, who tend to drive solo for most of the time. The rear tailgates give endless rust-problems; both upper and lower *will* rust and although not difficult to replace, neither is cheap, so look hard and bargain harder. In an ideal world, you will buy a car where both were replaced six months previously.

Inside

The trim was never of the best quality and the plastics in particular were very flimsy and easy to damage. Trim quality improved during the life of the S1 and more so for the S2, but Mercedes was never that worried by them. As such, a car where the interior trim is in good condition *and* undamaged is quite rare, not least since most owners don't bother to replace damaged trim on the grounds that the new part will probably last no longer than the original. The seat material is generally quite hard-wearing, but will probably be fraying round the edges on high-mileage examples. Similarly, plastic graining on the steering wheel and gear knob can smooth over when lots of miles have been covered.

Series 1 tailgates have a reputation that has passed into motoring folk lore. All you have heard is true – the upper tailgate rots all round and is expensive to replace. If you are faced with this prospect, consider upgrading to an aluminium-framed item. Similarly, water gets into the lower tailgate and rots along its lower edge, as can be seen here. Neither is particularly difficult to fit though lining up the pair of them can be very trying on the patience.

Although better than the Series 1, interior trim quality wasn't really up to the mark on the Series 2. Expect to find cracked and broken plastics and allow for replacement costs. This mirror trim would have to be replaced by a franchised dealer.

In terms of 'accessories', look for the most you can get for your money, with official Land Rover kit being preferred. The later the car, the more likely it is to have things we now take for granted – remember that the earliest S1 cars were around at a time when you were very flash indeed to have central locking!

Check the correct operation of all in-car electrics because replacements are expensive. This applies particularly to any security system fitted. Over time, Land Rover fitted their own systems, both immobilisers and combined immobiliser/alarms. Be sure that everything works and if there is a remote control, test it thoroughly – make sure you have the spare as well. If an aftermarket system has been installed, ensure it has been done professionally – DIY alarm fitments are not to be recommended. If the security is Thatcham-recommended, you'll need an installation certificate in order to convince your insurers who may then give away a little discount.

Air conditioning does add a premium to the car but make sure that it works properly – a thorough overhaul can cost well over £1,000. And remember, that when it is switched on, it will slightly increase the fuel consumption. Many owners realise this and turn it off,

but then the system goes to rack and ruin leaving the next owner to pay the huge bill for repair. Leather trim is a bonus but don't pay too much for it, as you can easily uprate this from specialists such as Nationwide Trim or by getting second-hand original equipment trim from a 4x4 breaker.

Underbonnet

The engine bay should look as if someone cares for the engine – if there's a layer of oily grime 10mm thick, it's time to go home. Not only has there been a careless owner, but it can cover a multitude of sins; massive oil leaks, cracked chassis, damaged coolant pipes etc.

Left: Early models had very little in the way of switches to press and gadgets to go wrong. This changed dramatically over the years, so it is vital to check that everything works exactly as it should.

Below: Air conditioning is very nice if you can have it – but only if it works correctly. Really put it through its paces, making sure it cools and heats exactly as it should. Remember, it can only be serviced and recharged by experts, who will charge expert money.

Check the oil, coolant, brake fluid and, where applicable, automatic gearbox levels. They should be spot-on and look fresh, which is always tricky to gauge on a diesel engine as the oil seems to go jet black almost immediately. Remove the engine oil filler cap and look inside. You don't want to see a white, foamy mayonnaise which could indicate a blown head gasket – an expensive operation on petrol or diesel. The steering box is a known weak point, so pay special attention here. The reservoir should be at the right level with no obvious leaks – it's an MoT failure point and replacement is expensive, wherever you buy. Check around the inner wings, which are known to rot through over time and look hard around the lower parts of the engine bay for signs of a front-end crash (creased metal, paint over-spray etc.).

Land Rover Tdi diesel engines

Before you lift the bonnet you need to know when the cam belt was last changed. The 200/300 series engines are prone to cam belt failure and the resulting damage as pistons and valves get together is extremely expensive. If there is no evidence it has been done recently, build the cost of a change into the price you pay – it is not a typical DIY job. Like any diesel, it will rattle more when cold, but it shouldn't vibrate overmuch, although a 300 engine should be less vibratory and slightly quieter than the earlier unit. Check the condition of all pipes and hoses, as they can often work loose over time. The Tdi needs its oil changing at least every 6,000 miles, something not all owners realise, so again, make sure you add this in to your estimate of running costs. You can use the idle test as a check on its general condition; let the warmed engine idle for a few minutes, then blip the throttle sharply, looking in the mirror (or with an associate standing behind the car). If you see great clouds of black smoke, it indicates trouble somewhere – possibly a tune-up will solve the problem but equally, it could be more serious internal engine wear.

V8 engines

As Chris Crane at RPi Engineering confirms, the most important servicing aspect of the Rover V8 engine is regular oil-changing. An engine which has had regular changes/filters will rumble happily on towards 200,000 miles. However, neglect this simple task and you're in trouble; sludgy oil deposits start to form which starts by messing up the cam and continues from there. Dip your fingers into the oil filler aperture (when the engine is cold!) and if they come out covered in black sludge, walk smartly away.

Transmission

Gearboxes

If you are not clued-up on how Land Rover products should work, it is advisable to take along someone who is. The gearboxes were never quiet and to anyone used to modern Euro-hatchbacks and their slick-shifting cogs, they can feel clunky and unrefined. Don't take gearbox problems lightly, as almost everything means removing the 'box which is a lengthy procedure. It isn't the sort of thing you can do on your driveway, or even in a well-equipped home garage. Of course, a worn/damaged/recalcitrant 'box can be an excellent bargaining point and if used correctly, can be your way to getting a good car cheaper, when gearbox specialists such as LEGS can soon sort out a replacement.

Manual

With the engine running and the car in neutral, and your foot off the clutch, listen for a gearbox rattle which could be a layshaft problem. There should be no baulking when selecting a gear and once engaged, gears should stay where they're put – check especially the lower two as they're the ones that get the most hammer and are most likely to jump out. Once engaged, there is usually a measure of noise, but it shouldn't be excessive. Look for an easy change from 5th to 4th gear – baulking here indicates some rebuild work as required.

To check for mainshaft or transfer 'box problems, pull up steadily, stop the car and engage reverse gear. As you let the clutch pedal up, listen for a harsh, metallic clack from the back of the gearbox – roughly underneath the driver's left elbow. If you hear it, there could be trouble ahead.

Automatic

Auto boxes should make progress smoother and less agricultural, with barely noticeable changes. All models were manual until 1982 when the already-ageing Chrysler Torqueflite three-speeder was stuck on to the back of the V8 engine – there was no diesel version at that time, of course. Its age meant that refinement wasn't a strong point, but conversely, it had proved itself behind thousands of hugely powerful American V8s and so was more than up to handling the, relatively, low output of the Rover unit.

The German-made four-speed ZF boxes fitted to Range Rovers after 1986 were much more advanced in all directions and have an excellent reputation for performance and reliability. Repairs can be more expensive than on the Chrysler 'box, but in both cases, major problems are usually glaringly obvious to anyone who has some experience. In practical terms make sure the engine will only start with the selector in 'P' (park) then select 1, 2 and 3 manually, driving some way in each to make sure that the gears are held correctly. Stop and select 'D' (drive) and drive some distance to ensure that progress through the gears is reasonably smooth and that you end up in top gear. Once there, hit the accelerator hard to ensure that the kick-down facility works properly. The Tdi engines always had to work hard with all that weight to carry and they had to work even harder with an auto transmission. This means that auto acceleration will seem rather dull in comparison with the manual gearbox.

There is invariably some degree of 'clunk' when selecting a gear or 'D' from rest, but it shouldn't be excessive. A reluctance to accelerate hard in any gear, a feeling like a slipping clutch, could be torque converter problems – not the end of the world in itself, but the gearbox will have to come out, at which point a general overhaul is also common sense, so there is a big bill coming – make sure it is not yours! Specialists such as Graham Whitehouse (Chrysler) or Ashcroft Transmissions Ltd (manual and auto) will be able to offer advice about repair, replacement or overhaul.

Low box
All Range Rovers have a second set of gear ratios, which are much lower than normal (i.e. a ratio of 2:1).

Above left: It is rare to find a Range Rover that doesn't have a coating of oil on its gearbox/transfer box or for that matter . . .

Left: . . . on the lower engine or differentials. You should not worry too much about a bit of a weep (as long as the oil levels are correct), but a constant drip, drip, drip makes a similar sound to a bank account being emptied.

Right: Suspension is fairly conventional (until the introduction of air suspension), with the coil springs and dampers being fitted which separate at the rear, thus making them easier to work on. With S2 cars, you can do little but monitor the physical condition; electrical checking requires a specialist with the right (i.e. expensive) machinery.

These are intended for serious off-roading or working in mud or snow. Low-box reverse is extremely useful for reversing with a large trailer. Make sure you check the low-ratio lever (the little stubby one on an S1; part of the H-gate on S2) engages correctly and that you can get the full complement of gears. This is important, because so many drivers don't use their Range Rovers as nature intended and so the second 'box is never used. Expect some reluctance to engage – remember the Land Rover gearbox is a large and complex collection of cogs and shafts – and be prepared for a little double-declutching to get there. If the centre differential lock is manual, engage that and ensure that the warning light illuminates – but only drive a few yards on tarmac, otherwise you will cause axle wind-up, which places extra strain on the drive components and chews the tyres up badly. You will usually have to drive a couple of yards after de-selecting the differential lock before you see the light extinguish – this is normal. Where the diff-lock is automatic, checking is difficult for the layman.

Suspension and steering
Range Rovers weigh over two tonnes which means there is a lot of car to support so dampers and springs

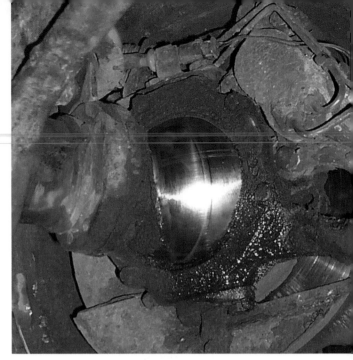

Left: Even without a ramp, you can get on your knees and check the condition of the steering swivel balls. They should be shiny, as here, with no signs of rust-pitting in the silver balls themselves. If there is, it indicates that they have been allowed to run dry of oil. Once rust has taken hold, the balls must be replaced, along with the seals which will be wrecked . . .

Above: . . . the result of which will look something like this. Replacement is a messy, fiddly job, not cheap and should always be done in pairs. Check Chapter Eight for details of how to avoid this by fitting flexible rubber gaiters.

need to be up to the job. Although all models will roll over more readily than a normal saloon (not least because of the extra height) it should still feel controlled and not uneven in anyway. The car should sit level all the way around, and if not, replacements are due. Down on your knees, check for signs of leaking from the dampers and if you see plenty of rust on them, they are clearly getting old.

Apart from the final few models, the Range Rover S1 suspension is fairly conventional, replacements are not expensive and there is a lot of choice from standard to seriously hard, but nevertheless, it is a bargaining point. While you are under the front of the car, look at the steering balls on each side, which should be oily on the parts where the steering can't reach and shiny silver where it can. Signs of rusting means they have been allowed to run dry and will need replacing, which is not cheap and quite involved to do. Later S1 cars and all S2 models were fitted with very clever electric/air suspension, which gives a much smoother ride. In addition, the driver can perform neat tricks, such as manually lowering the car for the benefit of passengers

getting in or out and for raising it to climb over obstacles that could damage the spoiler. However, it is a complex system where problems are far from unknown and setting-up requires some expensive diagnostic gear. Make sure that the whole system works absolutely perfectly.

Under the Range Rover is an absolute plethora of heavy-duty arms, links and rods designed to keep the car pointing in the right direction and these are supported by a series of rubber bushes. These bushes are weak points and by the time the car is, say, five years old, they will be well worn and ready for changing. If they have not been changed, swapping the lot can be a costly exercise, especially as it is not really a DIY job for many of the bushes as you would need a very capable bearing press for a start. If you are changing the bushes, it is well worth considering upgrading to Polybushes; these polyurethane replacements are far tougher, will last longer and will control the roll of the car far better than the original rubber fitments. Better still, good ones are a darn sight easier to fit.

Brakes

Stopping all that weight requires plenty of braking power. All models were equipped with twin circuit, servo-assisted brakes which work well regardless of model. Later S1 cars may be equipped with ABS anti-lock braking, which was an option for some years, and is fitted to the S2 as a matter of course. The brakes should stop the car quickly, without drama and without pulling to either side. (Bear in mind that veering around under braking could be down to worn rubber bushes mentioned earlier.)

The rear brakes in particular tend to get little use as most braking effort goes to the front. The result can be seized callipers, the best answer for which is replacement. Try to get a look at the discs and check their general condition. If there is a large lip around the edge, then the disc is very worn and probably due for replacement – of course, always replace discs in axle sets with new pads. Look around the callipers and at the brake pipes/unions in general for signs of fluid leakage. Check the operation of the servo by sitting in the car with the engine off and

Later Series 1 cars were fitted with Wabco ABS anti-locking braking. It is a useful accessory, but check that the warning light comes on with the ignition and goes off with the vehicle on the move. A light that stays on means expensive trouble – and no MoT pass.

pressing hard on the brake pedal. Start the engine and, as the servo kicks in, the pedal should go down noticeably. If it stays hard, then the servo is not functioning correctly.

Wheels and tyres

Alloys look better but are easier to damage and more expensive to replace. Official Land Rover wheels are favourite, as you can be sure they are up to the job of carting around such a heavy vehicle – which is particularly important when off-roading. Check around all the rims for signs of heavy kerbing, especially with alloys which are more expensive to repair/replace. Check the tyre tread and around the sidewalls, inside and out (another reason for having a torch on your checklist) – damage here can't be repaired and good tyres are not cheap. The tyres should be the same size at each corner (yes, really . . .) and ideally, the same type. A mix-and-match indicates someone trying to run the car on a shoestring; and if they're saving cash on this vital area of safety, where else have corners been cut? Cheap tyres are false economy and if those fitted are not recognised as being ideal for the car, build a set of (at least) four into your budget.

At the front, make sure that the tyres are wearing evenly. There is plenty of rods and joints under the front of the Range Rover, and all have to be spot-on to make the car handle and steer correctly. In addition, it is common for the pre-load on the front steering balls to be incorrect, causing wheel-wobble (often thought to be the fault of a perfectly good steering damper) and, of course, uneven tyre wear.

Left: Always try to get a look at the condition, and better still, the thickness of the discs and pads. They should have plenty of 'meat' on them. Rear callipers often seize because of their relative lack of use. When driving it is hard to tell, so physically checking to see that the pads are wiping the rust off the discs is the simplest way to check. As ever, look around the pipes, hoses and connections for signs of fluid leakage.

Below: A gentle probe under the length of the sills on both sides (ideally with gloved hands) will reveal any rot. Corrosion here is very common though, but there are plenty of repair panels available and in fact, the whole floor can be replaced if required – although it is not an easy job.

DID YOU KNOW?

In the cult TV series, *The Avengers*, archetypal Englishman John Steed drove a Range Rover – which in one episode was blown up!

Under the car

The S3 models broke with tradition and were designed with a monocoque body. However, all other models had a separate body bolted to a huge ladder chassis, two great box sections of steel running from front to rear of the car. Just about everything else is bolted to or hung from it, so it is vital that any rust is only on the surface. Check the two main rails and then the outriggers which extend at various points. The body bolts to these so it is important. A really weak area is the rear crossmember, unfortunate, as it is structural. Run a gloved hand right up behind the rear bumper (it's a dirty job) and prod hard with your fingers. This *can* be well-rotted even before the car gets to ten years old, so ignore this test at your peril. It can be replaced,

Above: In common with Series Land Rovers, Discoverys and Defenders, the water and muck sprayed up from the front wheels takes its toll on the foot wells. This is particularly nasty, but it is always a place to check. Usually, it can be patch-welded quite successfully or a proprietary repair panel can be fitted.

Above left: It is actually more important to check the condition of the rear crossmember, as seen here with the floor removed from inside the car. This one is truly rotten and it is very common to find this sort of rust damage. More usually, you would reach underneath the rear bumper with a thickly gloved-hand and press hard. Again, repair sections aren't dear, but it is a time-consuming task and requires lots of skill in the welding department.

Left: The rear floor edges are prone to rotting, particularly around the wheel arches where muck and dirt are thrown up against it. It looks worse than it is and with proprietary repair panels easily available, it isn't too hard for a good welder to sort out.

A blowing exhaust can usually be heard before it is seen. Check for obvious signs of blowing or damage. The front, double-skinned 'Y' piece on the V8 is a common place for rot to start.

but it is a very involved operation requiring an expert's skill – which means you pay an expert's money.

Look for rust/rot along the floors on each side, particularly the front arches and footwells and rear arches. As a rule, floors can be patch welded without too much difficulty and there are proprietary repair panels for just about everything under the car likely to rust.

At the rear of the car, early fuel tanks were steel which makes them prone to corrosion but they are not too difficult to replace and are relatively cheap. Later models and S2 cars were plastic and all but impossible to mend and are expensive to replace, but of course, they don't corrode, so they're usually less hassle. Of course, they're still vulnerable to off-road damage, so check just the same.

There's lots of ground clearance so there is no reason for not having a good look at the condition of the exhaust system. Make sure it is hanging correctly from the chassis hooks (they can rot quite easily) and that there is no sign of heavy rust or blowing from existing

holes or patched repairs. Remember that from 1993, petrol-engined Range Rovers had to be fitted by law with catalyst exhaust systems which are extremely expensive to replace and a good one is essential in order to pass the MoT test. One that's really shot will actually rattle, but often they can fail quietly. If the car has a long MoT then you might want to risk it. However, if it is due soon, then it would be worth asking the buyer to have it tested – even if you stump up the test fee, which is considerably less than the cost of the cat. Catalyst systems were optional on some V8s prior to that and if your car falls outside the legal-requirement date, you are quite in order to replace it with a standard exhaust set-up, which may not be quite as 'green' but it will be cheaper and it will free-up some power and torque. In addition, it gives the option of fitting a stainless steel system, such as those offered by Rimmer Bros, and thus removing exhaust replacement from your list of possible problems for many years to come.

Series 2

The basic rules of buying apply here as they did in the previous section – checking numbers on the V5, looking for poor paintwork and oil spills in the same way.

At the time of writing, the Series 2 Range Rover was

in that awkward stage of being technically obsolete, but not particularly old. As such, even one of the earliest models represents a hefty investment – albeit considerably less than its original selling price – while a recent model requires a very good relationship with Mr NatWest. The Series 2 isn't anywhere near as complex as the Series 3 in terms of clever electronic gizmos, but it is a world away from the Series 1, especially those early 1970s cars. Buying a used vehicle really does require the buyer to know what to look for, or to take along someone who does. If that's not you (or if you are still unsure) then either buy from a specialist dealer or a pukka Land Rover dealer. Both will charge more, but if it includes a decent warranty, it is worth it. If you buy a good Range Rover, you will enjoy it immensely and wonder why you ever bothered with a normal 'box on wheels'. Buy a bad one and you will just wonder why you bothered . . . Remember that there are many thousands of Series 2 Range Rovers for sale at any one time and you can afford to be choosy, so make sure you get exactly the model, specification and condition you want.

Build quality improved somewhat with the S2, but even with BMW's influence, it left much to be desired. Overall, it is generally thought that it took Land Rover until 1997 to really get everything properly sorted, so cars prior to that should be given even more scrutiny than usual. As a general rule of thumb for all models, start the engine and while it idles, ensure that none of the warning lights illuminate. The BeCM system will tell you of any fault.

Which model?

The petrol options were, of course, based on the venerable Rover V8, two capacities being offered, a 4.0 litre and a mighty 4.6 litre. When it came to oil-burning, the S2 cars switched from Land Rover's own diesel power plant to the six-cylinder, BMW unit. Taken in solus, the engine is fine and at the time of installation, had already done sterling service in the German manufacturer's saloon cars, albeit with another 10bhp. However, for lugging around 2-tonnes of 4x4, it was a little revvy and progress required more effort than many would have liked.

There were two versions of both the 4.0-litre V8 and the diesel DT models, a base/SE and DT/DSE respectively. The 4.6-litre cars were always badged HSE and had the top specification throughout the model run. The base models, if no extras were specified can seem rather lacking when compared with others in the range,

although taken on their own, they still have plenty to offer. However, the Range Rover is associated with luxury in the same way as BMW, Jaguar or Mercedes and as such, lower specification not only means a lower price *per se*, it also makes the individual car less desirable. The better equipped the car, the more desirable it is, which means although you will pay more, you will also find it easier to sell later on.

Special editions

Check back through Chapter Three and you will realise that there were plenty of special edition cars to muddy the waters of choice. In addition, the Autobiography programme means that it is quite hard to find any kind of standard vehicle. Make sure you are not buying a car that has just had an 'Autobiography' badge stuck on the tailgate; there should be a Special Vehicles identity plate on the engine bay slam panel. Some specials had lots of useful/expensive equipment on board which should make quite a difference to the price (notably such things as climate control, full leather interior etc.). However, a different paint finish and a few extra speakers in the sound system, shouldn't affect your wallet too much – if at all.

Engines

V8 petrol

The V8 engines (both 4.0 and 4.6-litre) are tried and tested units with an extremely long service record. They also benefit from some worthwhile updates on S2 Range Rovers, such as increased crank journal sizes and cross-bolted mains caps i.e. the mains caps are not only located by the original vertical pair of bolts, but also by an additional pair which run horizontally, through the lower block wall, and into the side of the mains cap.

The other major improvement, introduced on later Classic Range Rovers, is a crank-driven oil pump, incorporated in the timing cover. All these changes were designed to address some of the traditional weaknesses in the Rover V8 engine – and they work well.

However, some of the known V8 weaknesses are still there, particularly in the camshaft and valve train area (noisy tappets, rapid lobe wear on the cam, top-end sludge etc.) because these areas are virtually unaltered since the 1960s. This emphasises the need for owners to change the oil regularly – something to check during your buying negotiations. Also, despite the introduction of modern seals and gaskets in a major effort by Land Rover to sort the problem once and for all, oil leaks still occur! The worst affected areas are the 'valley' gasket (underneath the inlet manifold) and the oil pressure switch in the timing cover. Head gaskets are no longer the problem they once were, due to a redesign. However, a more serious problem can occur – particularly with the 4.6 – which results in coolant loss and overheating. The problem is caused by 'porous' block castings or block liner movement. The symptoms include overheating, coolant system pressurising and water in one or more cylinders. There is no simple cure for this and a replacement short engine is the only answer.

It is worth bearing in mind the GEMS (Generic Engine Management System) fuel system which is fitted to V8 vehicles. This is a modern, distributorless management system, governing fuel and ignition. As with most modern vehicles, it is generally very reliable. However, if a fault does occur, diagnosis and subsequent repair is not a DIY job as it requires sophisticated electronic equipment – and a large cheque at the end of it.

Also, from 1999, the V8s were massively revised under the 'Thor' project name, which bestowed improved power, torque and economy – but most of it was gained by using even more complex electronics, so even more care is required to make sure you don't end up paying a big repair bill.

Exhaust system

All Series 2 cars were fitted with catalytic exhaust systems (by law in the case of the V8-engined cars) and, unlike some of the S1 models, you can't junk the cat and replace it with a conventional system. Check it all very carefully, as these components, even when purchased at a specialist rather than a Land Rover dealer, are extremely expensive. The catalyst itself can be ruined by a backfire or by knocking it hard against a rock or high kerb (no real excuse here, of course, because of the clever suspension). Because the sophisticated electronics will automatically compensate at the engine, it is impossible for the driver to know whether the cat has failed or not – until the car is connected to the MoT station computer. If it fails, there's no MoT certificate until the offending article has been replaced.

Diesel

There is a definite difference here between the S2 and the earlier cars because the unit was not the Land Rover-developed Tdi engine, but rather BMW's well-respected in-line six-cylinder power plant. It had done sterling service in a number of the company's saloons and gained a good reputation thanks in no small part to its prodigious power and torque outputs and predictable reliability. Although generally very robust, the BMW engine can suffer from overheating, leading to head gasket failure. The problem is not helped by the design of the radiator, which has both the inlet and outlet hoses at the top. This design can lead to insufficient cooling. Make sure you run the engine long enough for it to reach full working temperature and keep an eye on the gauge.

Poor starting in a diesel vehicle can be caused by a failing fuel pump. This is relatively easy to check: look for air bubbles in the section of clear fuel pipe under the bonnet. If any are present, suspect the fuel pump. The pump is mounted inside the fuel tank and replacement requires removal of the tank – this is not a cheap or easy operation, so look beyond the mere cost of the pump itself. In addition, it is worth checking the oil cooler on diesel engine vehicles, as these have a tendency to leak.

Transmission

The four-speed automatic gearbox fitted to S2 Range Rovers is a well-proven ZF unit and was used very successfully on the Classic Range Rover models in a similar form. It is smooth in operation and extremely reliable. It featured the now common 'Sport' mode, which simply delays up-shifts until higher rpm. The manual gearbox fitted to certain models was Land Rover's own R380. This gearbox tends to be a little notchy in use, but is generally reliable with no major weaknesses. In essence, this means that if it doesn't work perfectly, then there is a fault requiring attention, and as most Range Rover gearbox problems mean removing the 'box, you need to balance the potential cost against the price of the vehicle – or possibly move on altogether.

The transfer 'box on all models is the superb Borg Warner chain-drive unit, with viscous-coupled, self-locking differential, again, these were 'run in' on the previous models from the late 1980s. These units are quiet in operation and immensely reliable and the big difference with the S2 Range Rover is the use of electrics in low-box selection. Gone is the old Hi-Lo lever, to be replaced on automatics with a single main selector lever which works in an 'H' pattern. Manual gearbox vehicles have a button on the dash for low 'box selection.

The key point on any gearbox – manual or auto – is to check that it operates on all the gears, high and low. With the luxury nature of the car, many owners will never have used the low ratio gears and at the other extreme, anyone who has done some off-roading could well have damaged them. An expert on hand is recommended, as the 'boxes are large lumps of engineering, despite the advent of electronics, and it can be difficult to know what is acceptable and what isn't.

As with all other previous Range Rovers, propshafts are of a conventional design and are reliable if greased regularly. Front axles feature open CV joints in place of the previous enclosed type – doing away with the heavy, complicated and high-maintenance swivel housings altogether – and are extremely reliable.

Bodywork and chassis

The bodywork of the S2 is a huge improvement over its predecessor, both in terms of panel fit and corrosion resistance. Corrosion really isn't a problem with these vehicles apart from one or two minor cosmetic areas; open the tailgate and check the inside of the bottom edge of the lower tailgate (where the outer skin folds over the frame) for electrolytic corrosion. Check the doors in the same way, and also the rear passenger door frame tops, where corrosion bubbles up underneath the rubber finisher. Another weakness is the numberplate lamps, which tend to fail frequently due to damp ingress.

In general, S2 Range Rovers will have been looked after rather better than their predecessors, as they cost so much more and tended to be sold to owners with deep pockets – for the first couple of owners, at least. Expect to find the odd ding or two in the bodywork – no-one can help it when someone else swings a door open on their car – but a really pockmarked car indicates a rather less than careful owner. Underneath the car, it is worth checking for obvious signs of rot and, although less likely, for evidence of careless off-roading. Particularly on early cars, check carefully under the rear of the chassis as there were rumours of towing brackets causing cracks in the chassis. This was reported to be because the rear lower spoiler necessitated the introduction of a swan neck towbar (rather than one which came out directly from the chassis as on the Series 1) and it acted as a lever to apply pressure to the chassis. Check this area even if a towing bracket isn't fitted – it might have been removed for the sale.

Brakes

The brakes on S2 Range Rovers are excellent; they incorporate a modern sliding calliper design, which is lighter, more efficient and less prone to fade than previous Range Rovers. Check the condition of brake pipes carefully – they commonly need replacing when the vehicle is a few years old and they are awkward to get to. The ABS system is an update of the Wabco system used in the Classic Range Rover and is similarly reliable, although, again, it relies heavily on electronics. Remember that for an MoT pass, the ABS light must illuminate when the ignition is switched on, but extinguish when the car is in motion. If it stays on, there's trouble ahead.

Steering

The design of the steering system is carried over from Classic Range Rover; it comprises a power-assisted steering box and drag link and track rod with replaceable ball joints, as before. The excellent ZF steering box is extremely robust and not prone to oil leaks. Drag link and track rod ball joints require frequent replacement, but are inexpensive and relatively simple to do.

Suspension

The suspension fitted to all S2 Range Rovers is an updated version of the ECAS (electronically controlled air suspension) system introduced on later Classic Range Rovers. It incorporates conventional dampers and bushes, but features air springs in place of coil springs. As well as providing better cabin insulation from poor road surfaces, the air bags also allow a variety of ride heights to be selected. However, as the name implies, the system relies on sophisticated electronics which, although generally reliable, are beyond the scope of the DIY enthusiast if they go wrong. Special equipment is required to set-up the relative heights of each corner of the car. A sure sign of trouble ahead is if the car is sitting lopsided on flat tarmac. Check the air bags inside each wheel arch for signs of cracked, split or perished rubber. Run the

The Series 2 car is packed with electrics and electronics so don't be abashed to try everything to make sure it works as it should. More importantly still, the brain for the BeCM resides underneath the driver's seat, leaving it vulnerable to water ingress on occasion. Even if everything seems to work correctly, check all around the area for any signs that there has been an excess of moisture here – mouldy, marked carpets for example.

suspension through its ride height cycles – it should raise and lower relatively quickly and without groaning or hissing noises. If it is slow, suspect a faulty compressor.

With the engine running, the handbrake on and transmission in neutral, manually lower and raise the suspension. On your test drive, the suspension should lower automatically into 'motorway' mode at around 55mph. When slowing, it should revert to standard mode at around 35mph and in both instances, the indicator light should confirm that it has done this.

Other front suspension components are conventional and long-lived, including radius arms, panhard rod

and anti-roll bar. At the rear, the traditional 'A'-frame was removed altogether and the radius arms made from a lightweight, glassfibre composite material which flexes and thus negates the need for a rear anti-roll bar. Suspension bushes last well and when worn, can be replaced with Polybushes, as per the S1.

Electrics

Electrical problems are by far the main area for concern with these vehicles, as virtually everything relies in some part on a box of electronic widgets. All interior and exterior functions are controlled by

DID YOU KNOW?

The 500,000th Range Rover was produced on 1 May 2002. It was an Epsom Green, Vogue 4.4 litre V8, its buyer was the then England goalkeeper, David Seaman. The supplying dealer was Chipperfield Land Rover in Kings Langley.

a large central control module known as the BeCM (Body electronic Control Module), which is located under the driver's seat. As with all such devices, this is particularly sensitive to damp – which makes one question the wisdom of mounting it so low in the vehicle. This is a fact worth bearing in mind if you are considering a car that has been seriously off-roaded or even one that has been flood-damaged. To that end, it is worth pulling off the plastic cover and checking the area around it – signs of damaged trim and carpet should ring alarm bells.

As well as controlling exterior and interior lighting, seat and mirror memories, electric windows and sunroof, wash/wipe features etc., the BeCM also communicates and interacts with all the other vehicle control units, such as the air suspension, ABS and engine ECUs. Any faults apparent with the BeCM will require proper diagnostic equipment and replacement of the unit at considerable expense. If you have any reason to suspect BeCM problems, don't be complacent, be afraid; be very afraid!

All Series 2 Range Rovers came with a remote-controlled alarm/immobiliser, with the top models having a more complex system which operates extras such as closing windows/sunroof. Make sure the car arms/disarms/operates the locking as it should and – absolutely vital – get both remote transmitters.

Interior

The interior trim, as with Range Rovers in the past, tends to be a little flimsy, although it is undoubtedly an improvement over its predecessor. Typically, in well-used and higher mileage vehicles, the driver's seat base collapses, the rear fold-down seat catches break, the glovebox catch fails and the bonnet release catch snaps off. Because this is pretty much standard across the board, it is not something to worry about too much, as long as you build-in replacement costs. Check all the electric windows, as the regulators are weak and often fail. On models equipped with automatic temperature control, check that the system works correctly and that no faults are recorded in the message centre. Problems

here revolve around the in-dash system itself and rectifying faults requires plug-in diagnostic equipment followed by expensive component replacement, necessitating complete dash removal. Check, too, that the air conditioning – if fitted – works correctly. If it doesn't, either the compressor or condenser may have failed and both are expensive items. Remember that just about anything to do with air conditioning (whatever its name) is a dealer job, because of the nasty gasses involved.

Series 3

A Series 3 Range Rover? Well lucky old you! The biggest problem you are likely to come across is trying to remember all those numbers in your Swiss bank account. By definition, the Series 3 cars are currently almost all on sale through franchised Land Rover dealers. It will be many years before they are common sights in the private ads or through specialists, and even then, great care should be taken, as the car is bursting at the seams with electronic wizardry, making the Series 2 models look like something conjured up by 'Blue Peter'. Replacing those innocuous black boxes full of silicon can cost mortgage money, so buying a S3 will always be a task to be undertaken with an expert on hand and some steady nerves.

One option increasingly being taken by UK buyers of new cars is that of personal import. In many cases, a British-built car can be purchased much cheaper on mainland Europe. We're talking many thousands of pounds here and with a car like the S3 Range Rover, the potential savings could be enough to buy another car with the difference. If you don't fancy the hassle and paperwork, a number of personal import companies exist and will sell to the UK buyer hassle-free. Clearly, the saving is less, but usually still considerable. Always make sure that the car you buy has *full* UK warranty and specification with a mph speedometer, headlamps that dip to the left etc.

Chapter **Seven**

Owning, running and looking after a Range Rover

Unlike other Solihull vehicles, such as the Series Land Rovers or even the Defender range, all Range Rovers are perfectly at home being used as 'everyday' cars – as at ease on the road as off it. At the time of writing, all Series 3 Range Rovers are still under warranty and being serviced by Land Rover franchised dealers. Even if they weren't, servicing one at home would be as sensible as trying to fettle a Concorde on your driveway. The S3 is never going to be one for the Saturday morning tinkerer. With just about everything being controlled by an ECU (electronic control unit), it is going to be down to experts such as Mark Adams of Pharmhouse Marketing, to sort out any problems.

The Series 2 car is something of a hybrid between the relative simplicity of the S1 and the moon-rocket

complexity of the S3. Essentially a longer S1 with more emphasis on electronics, there are quite a few areas where the DIY-er can get some dirt under his fingernails, but just as many where 'leave well alone' is the order of the day. As long as you know which is which, you'll be fine.

Maintenance
According to 'a bloke down the pub', taking on a Range Rover is akin to drawing out your life savings to burn instead of coal this winter. Of course, everyone's heard some horror stories, but that applies to just about every car you can think of. As with any vehicle, if you buy the right car to start with, you will find that keeping your Range Rover sweet can be very cost-effective. Most Series 1 Range Rovers are quite old nowadays, but happily, they are also rather old-fashioned, and low-tech is good news for those who like to do their own maintenance. Even if you don't, they are relatively cheap for a specialist to work on.

Tools and conditions
The Range Rover is a large, heavy-duty car which means you need sockets and spanners and other tools of the same ilk – a 3/8in socket set will soon wilt under the pressure. A few special tools are needed (the most obvious one being the large box spanner required for the front hubs – which is a worthwhile investment) but

It is hard to fully service your Range Rover without some heavy-duty tools to complement your existing set-up. A ³/₈in drive socket set and large spanners is a starting point. If you're really serious, go for some ¹/₂in drive sockets. (Teng Tools)

buy good quality at all times because you will invariably be applying lots of pressure to every nut and bolt and you need to know your ratchet is not going to strip a tooth at a vital moment.

One of the most common 'tools' you will need is a healthy stock of WD-40 or similar releasing agent. Rust gets just about everywhere and few threads will play the game once a car is a few years old – and the oldest Rangies are now more than 30 years old! Make a habit of smearing a dab of Copperease on each fastener you replace – including the wheel nuts/bolts; you'll soon come to appreciate the wisdom in doing this, especially if you're changing a flat tyre on the hard shoulder of the M6.

When raising your Range Rover for any reason, never forget that it weighs over two tonnes and will do you a power of no good if it drops on you. Take the matter seriously and use a good quality trolley jack with a large saddle to lift it – a bargain basement, £20 job isn't something I'd recommend – and *never* work under any car when the jack is the only means of support. Use good quality, decent-sized axle stands at suitable, solid points and use at least two every time. Where possible consider doing the work with the car with all four

Power tools make life much easier and air-tools are probably safer than electric in a garage environment – powered by a compressor you don't have to concern yourself with an electric cable trailing across the workshop (possibly falling into oil or coolant patches) and/or getting snagged or cut on bits of rusty bodywork. There's just about any tool you could care to think of and a few more you couldn't. Remember to wear eye and ear protection when using pneumatic tools.

wheels on the ground. If this isn't possible, check out any high-torque fasteners and see if you can 'break' them before raising the vehicle. It's forward thinking like this that could save your life.

Having dirty hands was once the only way to tell a real mechanic, but not any more. Oil has been found to be carcinogenic, so keeping your hands clean is important. Wear thin gloves if you can – vinyl and latex are the more common, but although the nitrile type cost a bit more, they are much more durable. If you can't, use a barrier cream before starting work. When washing your hands, use a decent cleaner which contains moisturiser to prevent them getting painfully chapped.

Keeping warm is vital when you're working on your Range Rover – if you start to get too cold, you will think

For safe Range Rover lifting, get yourself a large trolley jack with a 4in plus saddle (if it is much smaller than that, there is the risk the car could slip off). Always, but always, use axle stands. This Clarke pair is rated at six tonnes, which is reassuring, but more importantly, they're heavy duty, which means that they are better constructed throughout. Better still, their larger size means that you can raise your Rangie much higher without approaching the limit of their range.

Keeping warm is essential if you are to keep a clear head and not start rushing the job, especially in the UK where summers are notoriously short. A propane heater may be noisy, but it will provide prodigious heat both quickly and cheaply.

less clearly, start to make mistakes and find it difficult to do even the simplest things as your fingers go number. Even a modest propane heater will soon warm up your garage and make life much more pleasant – and safer.

V8 engine

The eight-cylinder Rover engine (used until the S3, which has a BMW unit) has been around for donkey's years and so there's a wealth of knowledge available and lots of outlets for spares. The key to keeping this lovely engine running sweetly is this; change the oil regularly! The engine is tolerant of just about all forms of use and abuse, but it will *not* stand being run with dirty old oil. A 10,000-mile oil change is maximum and fine if you do *lots* of miles in a year (where the engine/oil spends most of its time at the optimum temperature). However, if you're a low-mileage user (and many V8s tend to fall into this group because of the low mpg figures), then make that a 5,000-mile oil change. And, if you do a *really* low mileage, change it at least once a year. Without these changes, a thick, gungy sludge will accumulate and the camshaft will wear its lobes to nothing in double-quick time, leading to predictable engine problems – and expense.
All the metal shaved off the cam will find its way elsewhere with damaged main bearings following as night follows day. According to engine expert Holly at RPi Engineering, because the engine has its roots well beyond its first Rover usage in the 1960s, there is no need to go over the top with fully synthetic oils – a good quality 20w/50 will do nicely, which is more money saved.

Being all-aluminium, the engine doesn't take kindly to being overheated and will warp its heads at the drop of a hat, so always make sure the coolant level is topped up. Just as importantly, the coolant should be a 50/50 mixture of water and coolant* all year round, to prevent corrosion in the waterways, blockages and overheating. If the engine does overheat, you can expect warped cylinder heads, blowing head gaskets and possibly a distorted engine block. On older engines, it is worth fitting aftermarket Kenlowe electronic fans to supplement or even replace the unwieldy viscous unit. The latter can lock solid leading to gradual overheating problems, something to check if the water temperature gauge shows signs of overheating.

* Not anti-freeze anymore; modern coolant serves to lower the temperature at which it freezes and raise the temperature at which it boils – clever stuff.

If you have a Range Rover with a catalytic exhaust system*, then take heed! Cats are notoriously expensive to replace and unlike conventional exhaust boxes, don't have to be rotted through to be useless. They're relatively fragile and if you knock it hard enough, it can be wrecked internally. It shouldn't affect the running of the car because the engine management will compensate electronically, but when it comes to MoT time, the emissions will be way too high and a 'fail' is inevitable. Purchasing another will not be a happy occasion – at the time of writing, the official price was well over £1,000 – although you can often save a packet by buying from a specialist such as Rimmer Bros.

Diesel engines

Both the 200 and 300 TDi units are suitably tough for Land Rover installation. The BMW 2.5-litre unit, used in the S2 cars, is also a hardy engine, although its relative lack of low-down torque means that it tends to be revved harder than its predecessors. Both Tdi engines are prone to snapping cam belts and as this often leads to a completely wrecked engine, it's not something to be taken lightly. It should be changed at 60,000 mile intervals, although cautious owners often bite the bullet and knock 10,000 off that figure. If you have just bought yours and are unsure when the belt was last changed (if ever), invest in a new one. It's not an easy DIY fit so you'll be paying for labour as well, but balance the cost against that of a complete engine rebuild and you will soon see the reasoning. All diesels require regular oil changes at 6,000 miles and get very upset if overheating occurs, so always keep that 50/50 coolant mix topped up. Servicing an S1 at a specialist garage isn't that expensive and although service intervals are higher than the V8, remember that you are saving with every visit to the pumps and again by not having to contend with all those ignition components. Servicing costs for an S2 car are higher because of the increased complexity.

Electrical equipment

Most of the electrical equipment, such as electric windows, sunroof, central locking etc., is fairly conventional stuff. Faults are quite common, even in the late S2 cars, and are most likely to be due to component

failure. It is hoped that the S3 will at last deal with the unreliability spectre that has dogged Land Rover for many years. With any electrical item, always check the obvious things first, such as a blown fuse, wires coming adrift and of course, faulty earth connections. Substitution is advisable before replacing a component; for example, if an electric window won't wind up or down and the fuse is OK, try swapping the connections at the switch. If it works on another switch, then the original switch is at fault. If the original switch works a different window, then component failure is indicated. This sounds a bit involved, but it isn't really, especially when you check out some of the replacement prices. It is often feasible to get such parts from specialist dismantlers at a massive saving over the new part.

Drivetrain

Gearbox oil changes aren't as important as those for the engine and it's quite enough to follow the manufacturers' recommendations. You can do most good simply by using the 'box properly in day-to-day use, changing gear at the right time and using low-ratio for heavy duty work such as towing large loads and driving off the tarmac. One thing which will soon land you with a large invoice is using the manual differential lock (where fitted) while the vehicle is on a metalled road. You will get axle 'wind-up' very quickly and if you indulge too often you will soon be replacing various drivetrain components. The Range Rover uses old-fashioned propshafts which have several greasing points, front and rear. Happily, you can get underneath without raising the vehicle, so there's no excuse for not doing it. Just about every Land Rover ever made will have a permanent covering of oil around the front/rear differentials, and the main and transfer gearboxes. As long as this remains a light covering, with the occasional drip on to the driveway, there is no cause for concern. When you find yourself swimming in a lake of EP80, it's time to look more closely!

Neither the gearbox nor the transfer box lend themselves to DIY removal or repair – they're large lumps of metal and removal from underneath requires a large ramp and some specialist kit of the sort readily available by those who specialise in Land Rover 'boxes.

Steering

The Range Rover steering box is known for leaking, but there is little you can do other than making sure it always has enough fluid in the reservoir – running it dry is a sure way to wreck the seals and your bank account

* Some cars were fitted with cats as an option before they became a legal requirement. In these cases, their performance isn't measured the same way at MoT time and, indeed, they can be replaced with conventional exhaust boxes. Any vehicles built after 1st August 1992 must have a cat fitted.

at one hit. Check it when you check the coolant/oil/brake fluid levels and you should be OK. Look out for the first signs of uneven wear at the front tyres, which indicates some kind of misalignment, most probably tracking. Steering wheel shake as you drive over bumps could be the steering damper, but it could also be that the pre-load on the steering swivels needs adjusting. It is a DIY job as long as you have some time, a spring balance and a liking for working in bucket loads of oil!

Tyres

Good tyres aren't cheap so regular inspection is worthwhile. Check the pressures at least weekly and adjust for the type of driving – long sessions of high speed motorway work require higher pressures than playing in the mud. If you live in a rural area, where bad winter weather drastically affects the driving conditions, consider buying a set of deeper-treaded tyres on 'slave wheels' for winter-only use. The author uses road-biased tyres during the summer, on a set of stylish alloy wheels, with a set of MT (mud-terrain) tyres on standard steel wheels from November to March. When it snows in the Welsh mountains, it *really* snows . . . If you fancy going off-roading on a regular basis, the same principle will apply. S2 cars got much larger (and expensive) tyres to deal with increased power and on-road performance.

Suspension

The Series 1 suspension is conventional and so needs only conventional checks. Look for signs of oil leaking from the dampers, and having pressure-washed the underside of the car, look hard all around the springs for signs of cracking. Changing dampers or springs is relatively easy, especially at the rear where springs and dampers are separate. There is a huge range of choice from any number of specialists so you can mix and match to get exactly the ride quality you want. The S2 cars were fitted with electronic air bag suspension, which is not at all DIY-friendly and once part or all has been removed/replaced, it requires a boatload of special equipment to set it up. Once the sole province of Land Rover dealerships, many specialists now have this, and such competition has brought suitable reduction in prices, to the benefit of all owners.

Under the Range Rover's bodywork is a plethora of rubber bushes, there to keep things like radius arms, the panhard rod etc., all square. By definition, these wear out and an initially gentle ride turns out to be like a force 9 Atlantic crossing. Without doubt, the best way to address this is to replace them with polybushes – polyurethane items which tighten up the ride no end. Don't consider DIY replacement unless you have a four-post lift and some serious equipment.

Bodywork and chassis

Keeping the bodywork clean is a good move; use a quality car shampoo (never washing-up liquid, which contains the enemy of paintwork, salt) and rinse off well. With gleaming bodywork you have an opportunity to check for any accident damage or signs of corrosion – the most common form this will take is electrolytic reaction where steel and alloy meet.

Invest in a pressure washer and keep the muck and crud from building up underneath – vital if you go off-roading. Get into all the nooks and crannies, especially during the winter months when road salt will eat through the steel panels and even the chassis in double-quick time. It pays also to get plenty of anti-corrosion liquids under there, something like Waxoyl or Dinitrol. It's a messy, summer job but pays dividends. Keep a weather eye on the sills and floor panels, particularly the front foot wells which collect everything the front tyres throw back at them and they regularly rot through. Get to know a good welder – most welders rub their hands with glee at the sight of an approaching Land Rover owner. In general, it is possible to patch-weld most of the car's underside and although it is not the neatest solution, it is cheaper than replacing entire floor sections.

Interior

As we have already seen, Range Rover interiors improved over time, but have never been the best assembled or produced. Their fragility is just one of those things and all you can do is treat the inside carefully. Seats and shelves can be repaired or replaced quite easily and cheaply by specialists such as Nationwide trim. However, most of the plastic panels are Land Rover-only items and unless you can find something suitable in a dismantlers, you will have to pay top dollar for replacements.

Buyng spares

Spares from a Land Rover main agent are not particularly expensive compared with some 4x4s, but they are even cheaper from the plethora of specialist concerns such as Rimmer Bros – check out the pages of the Land Rover magazines for details of suppliers. In some cases, you can buy an original part in a different

Above: As Land Rover has moved ever more upmarket, it has left the way clear for knowledgeable specialists to sell both the cars themselves and a vast array of parts and accessories. In many cases, the parts sold are the same as Land Rover originals but in different boxes. (McDonald Land Rover Limited)

Below: Another excellent source of well-priced spares, second-hand bits and authoritative advice (both from traders and public alike) are Land Rover shows. The major magazines run their own and attending at least one a year is likely to pay for itself in 'show offers' alone, especially if you need to spend real money.

It is the simplest underbonnet task you can think of, but checking and changing the oil regularly will pay handsomely. This is especially so with the V8, which will soon ruin its camshaft if it is left to spin in dirty oil. And . . .

box and save lots of money, although in others, you will be offered a selection of different quality items; buy the best you can afford, especially when it comes to safety-related products such as brakes, tyres and suspension.

Security

Security is a big issue with any Range Rover; S2 models came with a veritable armoury of anti-theft measures, and indeed, won many awards for them. The S3 has gone one step beyond, meaning that the determined thief will probably have to resort to taking the cars with the keys already in (car-jacking) or stealing the keys from the house. Earlier cars however were not so well defended, indeed, it was only in the last few years that it became an issue at all. The locks are pitiful and present no barrier to the skilled thief. It is important to realise that any large Land Rover vehicle, let alone an upmarket Range Rover, is a valuable prize to the thief; there's a huge market not only for stolen cars (which take on a new identity – ringing) but also for spares – remember that the engine, gearbox and most of the running gear

will also fit the Discovery and Defender. A full description of security measures to take is given in Chapter Eight.

Regular checks

To get the most out of your Range Rover, and to keep it in tip-top condition, there are a few jobs you should do on a regular basis. We're not going to get into a 'How to do a full service' on your Range Rover, as that would take up too much space, and there's an excellent Haynes *Service and Repair Manual* (No. 0606) for the Series 1 Range Rover which tells you exactly what needs doing and when, and how to do it.

So, the idea of this section is to tell you what needs regular attention, and what to check to make sure that you are not let down by problem that could easily have been avoided. So often, one small item can be overlooked, only for it to develop into a bigger, and often more-expensive-to-fix problem.

Most of the items that need checking regularly can be found under the bonnet – you shouldn't even have to get your hands dirty!

The first and most important regular check is the engine oil level, ideally once a week. Always make sure your pride and joy is parked on level ground when you make the check, and wait at least five minutes after stopping the engine – to allow all the oil to run back into the sump – before you pull out the dipstick. Ideally, check it when the engine is stone cold. If you need to top-up, make sure you use good-quality oil, and don't overfill. Remember, though, that the V8 engine was designed in a different age and with different tolerances to the modern diesels and that all-singing synthetic oil is usually unnecessary – as a rule, a good-quality 20w/50 or 10w/40 is fine.

The brake fluid level should be checked regularly, especially if your Range Rover gets a lot of off-road use. It is just possible that if you have been driving over rough terrain you could have damaged a brake hydraulic line – not a problem that you want to discover for the first time as you fail to stop at a busy road junction! It is true that the car has dual circuit brakes, but the difference in braking ability when one of them is lost is massive. Brake fluid level will drop very slowly as the brake friction material wears, but you should hardly notice this, and any significant drop in fluid level indicates a leak somewhere in the system. In this case, don't drive the car until the problem has been found and fixed.

While you are under the bonnet, it's also wise to check the coolant level. The level is checked in the expansion tank, and should always be checked with the engine cold. If you need to top up, remember that using plain water is OK for an occasional top up, but if you do this too often, you will dilute the strength of the coolant, which will reduce its anti-corrosion and anti-freeze properties. Remember that a 50 per cent mix of

coolant and water is your aim; you can buy simple and cheap checkers from most DIY stores.

Keep the washer fluid level topped up – you can guarantee that if you don't the fluid will run out when you most need it, when driving on a salty winter road, or when following a tractor down a muddy lane! Add a reputable screen wash to help clean the screen and lower the freezing temperature.

Right, nearly there, just two more levels to check, namely power steering fluid and clutch fluid, or automatic transmission fluid, depending on whether you have a manual or auto model. The power steering fluid is checked using a dipstick attached to the reservoir filler cap. The fluid level should be checked with the engine stopped, and the front wheels set in the straight-ahead position. The only reason for the fluid level being low is a leak. As mentioned, this is a common problem although generally a weep will go for years before becoming serious – as long as the level is topped up regularly. To drive a Range Rover without power steering, you will need the physique of a body builder, so it's worth keeping an eye out for leaks! That physique will also come in handy when it comes to lifting the large wads of cash you'll need for

... while you can just about remove the cam with the engine in situ, it's not for the faint-hearted and if it is badly worn due to a lack of clean oil, there will be other problems stacking up elsewhere, not least ...

... worn main bearings. Compare the cost of oil and filters twice a year to that of a complete rebuild – no contest!

replacement parts – a few extra drops of fluid are far cheaper.

If you have a model with automatic transmission, the fluid level should be checked regularly as recommended in the vehicle handbook or manual. Nine times out of ten, automatic transmission problems are due to low fluid level. Finally, if your Range Rover has a manual gearbox, the clutch fluid level should be checked once in a while. Again, there should be no significant drop in fluid level during normal operation of the clutch, and any significant drop indicates a leak in the clutch hydraulic system.

That's all the underbonnet checks finished, but there are still just a couple more checks it is worth carrying out at least once a week. Check your tyre pressures – it's very easy to pick up a slow puncture if you've been driving off-road. Always check the tyre pressures cold, and if possible always use the same gauge to check the pressures – different gauges can often give surprisingly different readings. Try to get your own accurate gauge because forecourt gauges take a lot of mistreatment and are notoriously unreliable. Remember to include the spare, topping that up to 5–10psi more than is required, to allow for any change in pressure before it is needed; you can always let out a few excess psi.

One more check to go, and that involves the wiper blades. All that is needed here is a quick check to make sure that the blades are not split or damaged. It is worth renewing the blades once a year, even if they seem in good condition, as over time the blades tend to pick up grease from the road which will smear the glass, usually most noticeable when a car's coming towards you at night with the headlights glaring.

That's it! It should only take ten minutes or so to carry out these checks, but it is time well spent which will help you to pick up any problems before they develop into anything serious, and you will have the peace of mind that you shouldn't have any nasty surprises on your next epic journey, that could easily have been avoided.

Chapter Eight

Modifications

A sure sign that a vehicle has reached the heart of the 'enthusiast' is the number of modifications available. For the Range Rover, the list is seemingly endless, the pages of the specialist magazines being awash with advertisements for companies which can supply products and services aimed at making your Range Rover better in some way. These range from simple things like super-tough carpet mat sets and load protectors to complete engine and gearbox rebuilds. And that's before we start on Land Rover's own options catalogue! This chapter shows some of the more popular modifications.

Exhausting times
A stainless steel exhaust is a great investment if you're looking to keep your Range Rover for any length of time, and there's not much price difference compared to the Land Rover official parts. Fitting an exhaust system can be done on a DIY basis as long as you have reasonable facilities and plenty of patience. The most important aspects are: a) pre-assemble the entire system off the car, making sure everything fits easily – you'll be glad when you're on your back under the vehicle; b) don't fully tighten any of the component parts until it is all roughly in place, so that you can twist, turn and adjust to make sure it is not fouling or knocking on the bodywork. If you're not happy, invest a few extra pounds and let your local tyre/exhaust specialist do it for you; most of the fasteners on the original will seize and few of us have recourse to oxyacetylene kit which makes removal so much easier. And, of course, working with the car in the air on a four-post ramp reduces the time of the job enormously.

Reversing aid
Reversing your Range Rover isn't difficult, but the height of the lower tailgate can make it tricky to judge

There's a standard stainless system for most models that not only look good, but they sound better and last longer. (Rimmer Bros)

Above: This is the Rimmer Sports version, which allows the engine to breathe more easily than the original and adds a rather tasty rasp to that V8 rumble which is . . .

Left: . . . aided in this case by stainless-steel, tubular headers. Compare these with the original cast-iron monstrosities above, and you will see why the exhaust gas flow is much better, leading to increased power and torque throughout the rev range.

Below: And don't they just look great – shown here on the rebuilt, 3.9-litre engine – almost too good to cram under a bonnet.

the distance between yourself and the car behind. There's a large choice of electronic reversing aids around, all of which use sensors in or around the rear bumper (either one, two or four) which send a signal to a beeper or visual display in the car. These 'count down' as you get closer, and of course, you will get to make your Range Rover just a little bit more like the ultra-electronic Series 3 cars. However, remember this kind of device should be used as an aid, not a substitute for common sense and observation.

Hot stuff

Yes, your Range Rover already has a heater, but the Eberspächer unit does more than just keep your toes warm. Eberspächer is a name synonymous with vehicle heating and for the Range Rover enthusiast, one of the company's Hydronic pre-heaters is well worth considering. The device works on petrol or diesel engines and fits in the engine bay taking a tiny supply of fuel from the vehicle's tank. Working rather like a mini central heating system, it heats the vehicle's coolant, using a built-in pump to shift it around the engine. (Diesel versions also have a fuel pump.) There are several temperature safety devices to prevent it overheating, so you won't come out to find your pride and joy doing kettle impersonations.

The heater is controlled via a three-program, seven-day, mini-timer which is surface-mounted on the dash or wherever is convenient. It can be fitted instead of or as well as the mini timer. In terms of running costs, the Hydronic takes just 0.5 litres per hour and as it works from the vehicle's fuel system, it can be used anywhere. If required, the heater fan can be connected to the unit so that, if left switched on, it will blow hot air to the screen or car as required – a fully fused relay is used to prevent the possibility of electrical problems. In addition, there's the option of a remote control transmitter to switch it on and off manually.

There are several types of Hydronic system available, to suit both petrol and diesel-engined Range Rovers. The D4W is suitable for engines up to 2.5 litres, with the D5W being fitted to engines over that capacity. My thanks to John Jennings from Eberspächer (UK) Ltd for his help with the practical and technical aspects of this product.

The benefits of being warm

Starting your car with a warm engine greatly reduces wear on its internal parts – some 75 per cent of engine wear occurs in the first ten minutes as all that excess fuel required washes the oil off the bores. It means you start with no choke (or extra fuel from the injection system) so you save fuel which in turn saves both the planet and your wallet. If your Range Rover is a later model with a catalyst exhaust, you will benefit because the warmer the cat, the more efficient it is. The interior heater will work straight away and so warm the car and clear a frosty screen quickly.

In *really* cold weather (oddly enough, becoming more common in the UK as global warming takes hold), a standard engine will often not produce enough heat for the heater to work efficiently – leading in turn to misted windows. When this is the case, the Hydronic unit can be turned on manually whilst on the move to add a welcome warm boost. More importantly, it will be a comfort to anyone using their Range Rover in one of the more remote parts of the country, where winters are

The Meta Targa SR2 is one of the top reversing aids and is unique in coming with a special bracket to hold both the numberplate and the twin sensors. This means no messy exterior drilling or wiring and . . .

. . . when fitted, it's barely noticeable. The ECU is mounted just inside the rear load bay in a suitable position and the 'beeper', under the trim at the top of the 'D' pillar.

Left: This is the basic kit − minus the myriad of wires, connectors and fasteners.

Centre: Finding a location for the Hydronic unit itself is often the hardest part, although John reckons he's not been beaten yet. Certainly, there was plenty of room under this early V8 bonnet, but later models with twin batteries, air conditioning and all sorts of optional extras would have created more of a challenge. Series 2 cars present even more of a problem; in this case, the top of the nearside wing was chosen. Here, it's out of the way of rain and muck splashed up from below, and away from much of the engine heat.

Bottom: The timer control unit should be mounted somewhere it can be easily accessed and seen by the driver. In this case, it covered up a hole left by a previously-fitted electric sunroof switch.

harsher; as the Hydronic can be used to heat the car in the event of a snowy breakdown, miles from anywhere, it could literally be a life saver. Of course, if your bank balance can stretch to buying a Series 3 Range Rover, you will find a fuel-burning heater on the list of cold climate options.

Towing the line

Adding a towbar to your Range Rover makes it ready to do the job it is ideally suited for – towing. All diesel and V8 models make great tow cars, being the right layout – a wheel almost right out at each corner – with plenty of torque to cope with most loads and 4WD. Because the car is legally able to pull such large loads, you are well-advised to go for the German-manufactured (Oris), factory-fit towbar, which has been specifically designed to cope with the massive stresses and strains towing places on it. Better still, it will fit easily into existing holes which makes life easier.

Cosmetic surgery

There is plenty of choice when it comes to treating your Range Rover to a little light cosmetic surgery. Some of the products are purely for show and to make the car look a bit better, while others have some genuine purpose. Whatever, if you like it, fit it!

Side steps are a popular accessory fitment. They are seen by some as merely improving the looks although they are a genuine boon to those who are a little short of leg or are elderly/infirm. But remember that they drastically reduce the ground-clearance, meaning that serious off-roading is now off-limits and that when driving in deep snow or mud, the car will ground much earlier.

Rock and roll

The Range Rover is a tall, heavy vehicle which demands much of its suspension components. Series 2 cars have always handled better because of the controllable air suspension and standard roll bars while Series 1 cars, however, have often needed some attention.

Equally, all Series 1 and Series 2 models use a whole host of rubber bushes for the myriad suspension components and these wear gradually over time. Replacing them with Polybushes is highly recommended; there are now two types, a standard bush which gives a fairly soft ride (like the original rubber bushes) and a slightly harder type which tightens things up and is the author's choice on two different models so far. The polyurethane construction means they last much longer into the bargain.

If you haven't got anti-roll bars (front and rear) then fitting them is the next logical step. There are various manufacturers of proprietary kits as well as Land Rover's own. All will need fixing plates welding to the

The kit contains everything you need to complete the job – except a few spanners. There's all the nuts, bolts and brackets, a pair of gloves to keep your hands clean when you're hitching up and even a sachet of grease for the towball!

The two arms and rear towing ball plate bolt together like this. The plate bolts to the underside of the rear crossmember and the arms are bolted into existing holes (for the tie-down loops) in the chassis members.

Above: A typical step of the sort available from Land Rover itself or just about any of the aftermarket accessory companies. Most simply bolt into place with perhaps the odd hole to be drilled in the main chassis members. They're quite an easy DIY fitment.

Left: They are also available for the Series 2 models, albeit they have been styled with a bit more care – note how they blend into the lower front and rear wheel arches. (Rimmer Bros)

Below left: Bull bars remain a contentious issue, although many options for the Range Rover are now padded, as here. It is important to notify your insurers if you fit one, as they are universally getting the jitters about huge pedestrian claims. Note also the matching lamp guards. (Rimmer Bros)

Below: An inner load tray like this is a really useful product if you make good use of all that luggage space. It protects the original carpets and stops the loads rolling around because of the large lip. It's easy to fit and remove when not required. (Rimmer Bros)

front and rear axles, so unless you're a real wizard welder, it's a job for the professionals, not least because of the accuracy required. Choosing the right dampers and springs requires some input from a professional who knows the business; the 'right' equipment for the enthusiast off-roader is seldom the right choice for motorway-man. As a general rule of thumb, the typical driver would benefit most from a set of relatively (or totally) standard springs, with uprated dampers to keep things under more control. These, plus anti-roll bars and Polybushes will make for a very controlled ride and steady handling without being sponge-pudding soft or teeth-rattlingly hard. Replacing springs and dampers is a fairly simple DIY job as long as you have sufficient heavy duty kit at hand, notably a high-quality trolley jack/axle stands and a tough, ½in drive (at least) socket set, capable of shifting fastenings which will doubtless be somewhat recalcitrant.

Fitting Polybushes

It is not really a DIY job unless you have access to lots of expensive equipment. Although some of the original bushes wouldn't be too difficult to sort, some of the securing bolts will undoubtedly be very reluctant to leave home. The torque required can be extreme and impossible to apply with the vehicle simply jacked up on the ground.

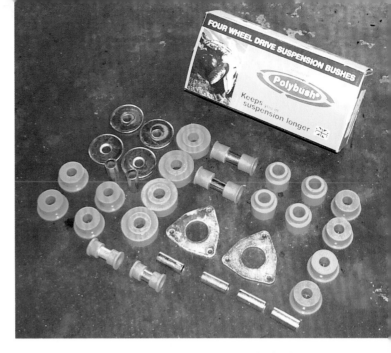

Polybush sets usually come in two types, a classic somewhat harder bush coloured red, and a slightly softer 'comfort' bush, coloured blue. These orange versions of the classic bush were produced specially for Scorpion Racing, to match their own anti-roll roll bar dampers and springs.

Here you can see a direct comparison between the Polybushes and the original (at top right). Note that the new bushes are in two halves, one reason they're so easy to fit. However, getting the old bushes out is another thing altogether – most will need a hydraulic press and around 15 tonnes of pressure. They are generally not the sort of thing you can sort with a hammer and a bit of brute force!

Above: This is a front anti-roll bar fitted by Scorpion Racing. The bar itself is their own design and manufacture, although they use Land Rover's fitting kit. In essence, the installation is not difficult, although many of the fasteners will have rusted solid and require a great deal of torque to remove them. This means high quality tools and having the car safely off the ground – if you don't have both, go to a professional. This applies even more so when it comes to the welding of the brackets to the axle casings. They have to be fitted in exactly the right position and seam-welded for strength – not a job to practise on. The finished job, not only looks pretty in Scorpion orange, but massively improves the ride quality of the car.

Fitting uprated springs and dampers

Fitting dampers and springs is within the reach of most keen DIY Range Rover owners and good quality products are not difficult to find. As well as suspension, uprating your brakes is never a bad idea.

Fitting M.A.D. interactive suspension

Retro-fit airbags? Yes, but perhaps not as you might think, because the M.A.D. bags are actually incredibly tough polyurethane units which fit inside the rear coil springs of a Series 1 Range Rover. Air pressure is added (either from an external air line or from an optional on-board compressor) to compensate for the extra stresses and strains applied when carrying heavy loads or when towing. This works to great effect and gets rid of that tail-heavy attitude which can lead to steering, braking, lighting and general handling problems. When not required, the air pressure is released and the suspension reverts to standard. The system automatically monitors the pressure and pumps it to the minimum (5psi unloaded) should it drop too low. A heat shield is always fitted to prevent heat from the exhaust affecting the airbags. They don't interfere with the normal running of the car but are enormously useful when there's lots of weight to be carried or towed. This Dutch system is imported to the UK by Klann tools and my thanks to Clive Berry and Wim Nells from M.A.D. for their help in compiling this section.

Finding your way – GPS (global positioning system)

My thanks to Garmin (Europe) Ltd for their help with this section.

This shows a set of dampers and springs from **Scorpion Racing** ready to be fitted. According to Scorpion boss, Colin Aldred, a common mistake is for owners to fit the heavy-duty springs at the front and the others at the rear. The result of this is that the car not only looks ridiculous, with a massive nose-up stance, but handles dreadfully. Remember that most of the weight is generated at the rear of the vehicle, especially when loaded-up or towing.

Fitting at the rear is easier than the front, because the dampers and springs are separate and there are no engine-bay components to get in the way. However, if you have an anti-roll bar, it will have to be released to allow sufficient axle movement.

You don't have to be trekking across the Sahara to find GPS useful, it can come in just as handy on a Sunday afternoon green-laning session or a harassed Thursday drive through Wolverhampton town centre. But what is GPS? It is a satellite-based navigation system made up of a network of satellites placed into orbit by the US Department of Defense. Originally intended for military applications in the 1980s, the government has allowed the system to be available for civilian use. GPS works

Left: This is the basic M.A.D. suspension set-up, comprising the airbags, tough polyurethane spacers and the plastic tube which connects the airbags to the supply. Normally, the bags would be topped up using a small compressor or a garage air line, but a neat 12V on-board compressor is available to make it more convenient.

Above: This shows how the airbag fits inside the spring with the protective polyurethane spacers at the top and bottom. The one at the top has a hole in its centre which keeps the air feed tube, which passes through it, free from harm. The tube has to be routed carefully to avoid being cut, burned or snagged.

Left: Rossini brake discs are said to improve stopping distances by as much as 40 per cent and heat dissipation is improved by the use of new steel compounds, notably by increasing the magnesium content. This enables them to lose more heat, more quickly. In addition, the discs have been made stronger by using a combination of chromium and titanium. Drilling the discs also helps get rid of heat and increases instant brake grip while the grooves reduce brake pad glazing and repel brake dust and moisture.

in any weather conditions, anywhere in the world, 24 hours a day. There are no subscription fees or set-up charges to use GPS. What else is so useful and free?!

A total of 24 GPS satellites circle the earth twice a day in a very precise orbit some 12,000 miles up and travelling at 7,000mph. GPS receivers pick up this information and use triangulation to calculate the user's exact location. Essentially, the GPS receiver compares the time a signal was transmitted by a satellite with the time it was received. The time difference tells the GPS receiver how far away the satellite is. With distance measurements from a few more satellites, the receiver can determine the user's position and display it on the unit's electronic map. Each satellite transmits an identification code which is available on many of the more modern receivers.

A GPS receiver must be locked on to the signal of at least three satellites to calculate a 2D position (latitude and longitude) and track movement. With four or more satellites in view, the receiver can determine the user's 3D position (latitude, longitude and altitude). Once the user's position has been determined, the GPS unit can calculate other information, such as speed, bearing, track, trip distance, distance to destination, sunrise and sunset time and more.

Today's GPS receivers are extremely accurate, thanks to their parallel multi-channel design. Most modern receivers have 12 channels or more and lock quickly onto the available satellites. In general, it takes a lot to totally block out all the signals being received and so they rarely lose the position. It's fair to expect an accuracy of 15 metres or better.

Aftermarket

GPS systems are ever more common, especially in top-of-the-range models where they're usually built into the dash on the production line; the Series 2 was the first Range Rover model to have this, a CARiN system in a special edition in 1997. But there are plenty of options for those of us who have to buy older cars, probably the top aftermarket choice being a DIN size unit which fits in the aperture left by the standard radio/cassette. The screen unfolds electronically and all the electronic boxes and wiring looms are hidden behind the dash. The main downside is the cost, complexity of installation and the fact that much of the rest of your audio system has to be added separately. In addition, the unusual radio position in all S1 cars, makes this tricky. Another option is to fit a stand-alone satnav system, where the CD-ROM (which holds the digital mapping disc) is hidden and a separate screen is mounted on the dash. This means that the existing audio system can be left alone, although for some, the inconvenience of having the screen sticking out on the dash is too much hassle. In addition, it can represent a security problem, being a real temptation for a thief, so some sort of quick release bracket is essential.

The third option is a portable satnav device, many of which now come with cigar-lighter connections enabling them to be used for long periods of time in-car. The advantage with these is that they can be used

The completed unit is shown here in situ.

away from the car – ideal for a spot of backpacking – and, of course, they can be transferred to a second car. They lose out slightly in terms of overall accuracy because, unlike permanent fit systems, they aren't connected to the vehicle's speedometer, so when the GPS signal is lost (passing under bridges or heavily wooded areas) then everything stops until it can be regained. The GPS antenna can be either built-in, as with portable devices, or a separate, plug-in device. They can be hidden beneath plastic trim, but they cannot 'see' through metal.

Of most use to Range Rover owners are those which contain road mapping information, allowing easy route-planning on a day-to-day basis, as well as a grid reference, particularly useful when going off-roading where being in exactly the right place can be the difference between law-abiding and law-breaking. While getting totally lost on a UK green lane is unlikely, it does mean that should trouble strike, you will have an exact position to relate when you phone for help.

Above: VDO is well-respected in the field of satnav. Like most road-based systems, the screen shows mapping information taken from a CD-ROM hidden away. A GPS antenna picks up the signals and an electrical feed from the speedometer helps keep track still further.

Below: The Garmin StreetPilot is an excellent option, working from the cigar lighter while still providing a full-colour screen with spoken instructions. The mapping information is downloaded into the unit from any PC computer.

These are the most popular Land Rover wheels for the Series 1 Range Rover, namely the Cyclone, Vogue, Sports, Freestyle, and styled LSE, and are available from Land Rover and companies such as Rimmer Bros. (Rimmer Bros)

Wheels

Early S1s were fitted with 6J Rostyle steel wheels with no options until the advent of the three-spoke Vogue alloys in 1981. Those early cars *cannot* take alloy wheels even though the PCD is the same, as the studs aren't correct – alloys can only be fitted if the studs have a triangle stamped in the outer end. This aside, wheels are interchangeable between the S1 Range Rover, S1 Discovery and Land Rover Defender/90/110 vehicles.

Left: For the Series 2, there's the Hurricane, Triple Sport and Mondial. (Rimmer Bros)

Above: Not wheels, but specially drilled spacers. Fit these to your Series 1 model and . . . (Rimmer Bros)

Below: . . . you'll be able to fit some of those stylish wheels originally fitted to the Series 2. (Rimmer Bros)

Trim

As we have seen, Range Rover trim has never been the best quality in the world and, like everything else, it wears out over time anyway. Enter Nationwide Trim a company able to revitalise or replace most seat/trim items with either standard items or some rather special alternatives; leather in a whole host of colours is a favourite for those wishing to make their Range Rover something special. Another product to look out for is their rear seat conversion, enabling an early car to be converted with a two-piece, split folding rear seat arrangement.

This is one of Nationwide Trim's demonstration vehicles, looking every bit as good as an Autobiography – but would you really want to fill up the back with hay if it looked like this?

Nationwide has a full trim restoration service and you can select virtually anything like, though . . .

DID YOU KNOW?

If you have a V8 with a flashing oil pressure light, it is not necessarily a big bill looming. Whilst it could be lower pressure caused by worn big end bearings with a large bill heading your way, it is more likely the oil pressure switch itself which is faulty. It is a simple, five-minute DIY fix and as it costs around £5, should always be tried first.

check all four tyre pressures at the press of a switch and without leaving the car is luxury indeed – as well as adding to the safety of the vehicle and its passengers.

Swivel housing gaiter

Having read about swivel balls in Chapter Six, you will know that lack of oil and attention mean lots of expense. One way to avoid this is to fit Bailcast gaiters. The company has been making this kind of neoprene rubber cover for years and has, at last, seen that Range Rover owners (or any Land Rover vehicle with this kind of steering arrangement) can benefit, too. The gaiters are split, so there's no need to remove the wheel which makes installation remarkably simple. Once in place, a bonding agent is applied with a metal strap retaining the gaiter at either end, then the conversion is completed by using the GR130 swivel housing grease instead of conventional oil. It is suitable for all Range Rover models up to 2001 model year. The semi fluid grease withstands shock loading in oscillating joints and is highly resistant to water and salt corrosion. It lubricates swivel pins, joints and housing

Left: . . . leather trim is an extremely popular choice.

Below: The SmarTire pack includes the four sensors and display of your choice – there are various selections, from basic to 'full monty'.

SmarTire

Knowing your tyre pressures are correct is a vital aspect of road safety, particularly for those owners who go off-roading and are likely to lower the pressures for muddy conditions. We all know they should be checked on a regular basis, but they're easy to forget – unless you have some electronics to hand. With the SmarTire system, small sensors are strapped to the insides of the wheel rims and they are triggered by centrifugal force applied by the rotating wheels. The signals they send are picked up by a small console mounted inside the car. From this, the owner can check the pressure – and temperature – of all four tyres at any time. More importantly, if a pressure drop of 6psi is detected, an alarm sounds. In addition, a temperature alert sounds if the tyre gets above a preset temperature. The ability to

Above: This is the more complex of the displays, with LEDs which show that each sensor's signal is being received and, at the press of a button, the current temperature and pressure. Again, this is the type of state-of-the-art accessory available on the Series 3 Range Rover.

Left: The sensors are light, but startlingly tough.

DID YOU KNOW?

No matter how gentle the off-road manoeuvre, remember that you should always keep your thumbs on the outside of the steering wheel. If you don't and there's a sudden kickback – say where a tyre drops into a rut or hits a large obstacle – the rapid spinning of the steering wheel could seriously damage your fifth digits!

seals, protects spheres and the one-shot container gives filled-for-life protection. This is a very useful product indeed, as recognised by Land Rover itself which produces a similar version under part number STC3435.

Security

Whether your Range Rover is heavily modded or totally standard, it is a tasty prize for the thief. Because of the way that Land Rover products (up to the S3 cars) can be pulled apart and parts interchanged, they are highly prized. Equally, many of them find their way to foreign markets. Over the years, standard-fit immobilisers became common and latterly, compulsory – Series 2 cars in particular have much-improved security systems. Depending on the model, an integrated alarm may also have been fitted. If you have no security, then an immobiliser is the least you can do. Fit an alarm with it for more peace of mind and when you link it into your electric windows and central locking, you will have the convenience of single button locking/alarming, together with a screaming siren to warn of intruders.

Above right: Your wheels and tyres represent a good night's work for the thief. Fit locking wheel bolts to add some grief to his life. Remember that alloys and steel wheels have different fitments.

Below: The gaiter kit and swivel housing grease. Fitted correctly, they completely seal against dust, water and grit and come with a two-year guarantee.

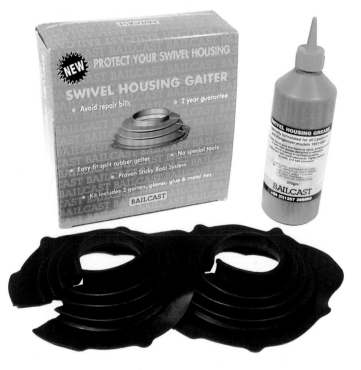

Because electronic security systems have become ever better over the years, more cunning thieves take a side-step to stealing your vehicle by breaking into your house (often much less well protected than the car) and taking the keys. Worse, car-jackings are on the increase, where a thief will take the car with the keys in the ignition and engine running, say, for example, when the driver gets out to open gates. The nastiest form of car-jacking occurs where a driver stops the car and the thief enters and threatens the driver. It is circumstances such as these which have been the catalyst for a large number of tracking systems – if you have a particularly valuable Range Rover, you are well advised to consider one, because if your car is stolen you will always know where it is and, more importantly, so will the police.

The true costs

The true cost of having your Range Rover stolen is far more than you would at first imagine. First, there is the inconvenience of having no vehicle – taking 'public' transport is expensive and awkward, hiring a car is incredibly expensive. And as a car is only declared 'stolen not recovered' after 30 days, that is a whole month's inconvenience to start with. Then there's the haggling with your insurers over the value of the vehicle. This can be protracted and almost always leaves a deficit to be made up by the owner in order to replace the vehicle with one of equal standing.

The excess – the first amount of any claim paid by the insured – can be as low as £50, but is usually much more than that, in some cases as much as £500.

Then there's the matter of no-claims discount (NCD). Most companies set the insured back two years NCD for a claim, usually 20 per cent. Add one fifth to your last year's *gross* premium to see how much difference that

Above: Most alarm systems comprise a siren, main ECU which controls everything, ultrasonic sensor for interior protection, twin remote control transmitters and a huge wiring loom. This particular model has the option to add-on an anti-hijack button – increasingly important nowadays. In many cases, it is possible to link the remote transmitters not only to the central locking, but also to electric windows and electric sunroof – all of which adds to its everyday convenience. (MetaSystem UK)

Below right: Sorting out a veritable morass of wiring is one reason that alarm fitment should be seen as a job for a professional. The safety aspect should never be overlooked, especially with later cars getting ever more complex electronically. (MetaSystem UK)

would make. And don't forget that while you go *back* 20 per cent, you only go *forward* 10 per cent per year, so you are penalised for *two* years. In addition, the insurers could impose special terms if they feel the circumstances of the claim demanded it.

For drivers with a suitable driving history, it is often possible to 'protect' the NCD. However, insurers are always at liberty to refuse to offer reinsurance to anyone they feel is an unacceptable risk, and any other insurer will penalise you for your claims history. All this is expensive and inconvenient and is the reason why you should secure your Range Rover – now!

Basic rules

* Park sensibly – down a dark alley is asking for trouble.
* Don't leave valuables in the car, especially credit cards, cheque books etc.
* If you have installed an alarm, use it! It's surprising how many don't.
* If you must leave anything in the car, put it out of sight.
* Lock your Range Rover whenever you leave it, even in the garage.

* Don't relax at home; a huge proportion of thefts occur at or near the owners' home.
* Take the ignition keys in the house and put them somewhere not obvious – most keys are within 6ft of the front door – something also known by the thieves who steal them.

It's a gas

It is one of the great Range Rover quandaries – you want the torque, power and offbeat rumble of that lusty V8, but the thought of feeding its petrol habit makes you quake in your boots. The answer is LPG – liquefied petroleum gas. Convert your Rangie to run on LPG (while retaining the petrol-power option) and you will be running on almost half-price fuel. Better still, it's a 'clean' fuel in terms of exhaust emissions, and because it burns so cleanly, it is better for the engine, too; oil stays cleaner for longer and spark plugs look almost new after 10,000 miles. Finally, LPG is actually a 'waste' fuel – that is what you see burning off the top of oil derricks. As such, it is effectively free (given that there's still a demand for petrol and diesel) and moreover, when it's burned through a catalytic exhaust, it pollutes the atmosphere far less than burning it 'raw'. Obviously, there's a cost to convert, but it's about a third of the cost to change the engine to a Tdi diesel unit, which makes plenty of sense when the LPG car will do the same – or more – mpg by price.

As a vehicle fuel, it is actually far safer than petrol.

Above: These are the basic components required for a standard LPG conversion to a fuel-injected Range Rover. Two small black boxes (emulators) plug in-between the fuel-injectors themselves and the car's ECU so that it is fooled into thinking the car is still running on petrol. If these weren't present, the ECU would shut everything down as the system switched from petrol to LPG. (Iwema Enterprise)

Below: The engine bay of this 3.5-litre, EFi engine is a typical LPG conversion. It's busy, but not much is actually the LPG equipment. (Iwema Enterprise)

There are lots of different types of tanks with varying locations. This is a simple spare-wheel well location for the Series 2.

This is a twin tank (note the tube linking them together) which fits in place of the original fuel tank, and . . . (Iwema Enterprise)

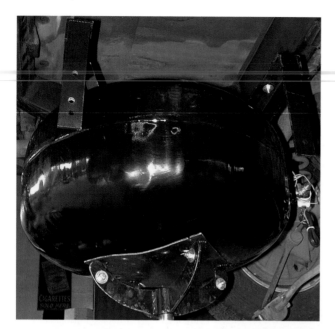

Left: . . . this single, round tank fits in the same place. Where the original petrol tank is removed altogether . . .

Below: . . . a stainless steel replacement is fitted under the rear wing. This uses the original filler, pipes and gauge sender.

Opposite above: France is a great place for any Land Rover enthusiast, not least because there's hundreds of miles of off-roading to go at. And the French love their Rangies – they even race them! (Nick Dimbleby)

Opposite below: Even using the diesel-engined Range Rover in the Camel Trophy Madagascar in 1987, couldn't help its reputation. The Italian VM engine was eventually ditched for a home-brewed version. (Nick Dimbleby)

The gas is kept in a massively strong tank which is typically around four times thicker than the average fuel tank. Three solenoids within the system check for leakage and if one is detected, they instantly shut off the flow of gas. When filling, the gas is pumped in under pressure and so, unlike petrol, you can't get spillage all over the forecourt – and your shoes.

The downside is that you have to find space for the LPG tank, but there's so much choice around nowadays, there has to be something suitable for just about everyone.

It is important to find high quality equipment, designed specifically for your Range Rover. Just as important is to have it installed correctly; using a true professional is probably cheaper in the long run and he will also have the right equipment for setting up the system correctly – not something that can be done by guesswork.

Specifications

Range Rover Series 1 (1970–1996)

ENGINES

Petrol	Capacity (cc)	Bore x stroke (mm)	Power bhp @ rpm	Torque lb ft @ rpm	Compression ratio
V8 3.5-litre (1970–9)	3,528	88.9 x 71.1	132/5,000	186/2,500	8.13:1
			130/5,000	185/2,500	8.25:1
			135/4,750	185/2,500	8.5:1
V8 3.5-litre (1979–81)	3,528	88.9 x 71.1	125/4,000	185/2,500	9.35:1
V8 3.5-litre EFi (1985–89)	3,528	88.9 x 71.1	165/4,000	206/3,200	9.35:1
V8 3.9-litre (1989–92)	3,950	94.0 x 74.1	188/4,750	235/2,600	9.35:1
V8 3.9-litre (1992–95)	3,950	94.0 x 74.1	181/4,750	231/3,100	9.35:1
V8 4.2-litre (1992–95)	4,278	93.98 x 77	200/4,850	250/3,250	8.94:1

Diesel					
VM 2.4-litre turbo diesel (1986–89)	2,393	92 x 90	112/4,200	183/2,400	22.1:1
VM 2.5-litre turbo diesel (1989–92)	2,498	92 x 94	119/4,200	209/1,950	22.5:1
2.5-litre Tdi (1992–95)	2,495	90.47 x 97	111/4,000	195/1,800	19.5:1

TRANSMISSION

The main gearbox was the four-speed LT95 until 1983 when the LT77 five-speed 'box was introduced. This in turn was replaced by the LT77S in 1991. The R380 was used from 1994.

The Chrysler Torqueflite A727 three-speed automatic gearbox was available from 1982.

The four-speed, ZF 4HP22 automatic gearbox replaced the Chrysler version in 1985.

SUSPENSION

Front: Coil springs. Axles located by radius arms and Panhard rod. Non-adjustable telescopic, double-acting dampers.
Rear: Coil springs. Axles located by radius arms, support rods and central wishbone assembly incorporating Boge Hydromat, gas-filled self-energising ride level unit. Non-adjustable telescopic, double-acting dampers.

STEERING

Burman recirculating ball, worm and nut type, incorporating an AC safety column with security lock. Non-assisted until 1973 (optional).

BRAKES

Lockheed servo-assisted disc brakes. Dual circuit system for emergency braking to front wheels only. Expanding drum type hand brake working on transfer box rear output shaft.

Front: 11.75in front (four-piston)

Rear: 11.42in rear (two-piston)

WHEELS AND TYRES

Rostyle 6J x 16, five-stud steel wheels with 205 x 16 tyres

Three-spoke alloy wheels 6J x 16 optional from 1981. An increasingly wide range of 7J alloy wheels available from then.

VITAL STATISTICS

Dimensions (mm)	Standard Range Rover	Vogue LSE
Wheelbase	2,540	2,743
Track	1,480	1,480
Ground clearance	190	190
Overall length	4,470	4,648
Overall width	1,780	1,780
Kerb weight(kg) (four-door)	1,723	1,986

Range Rover Series 2 (1994–2002)

ENGINES 1994–1999

Petrol	Capacity (cc)	Bore x stroke (mm)	Power bhp @ rpm	Torque lb ft @ rpm	Compression ratio	Manual gearbox	Auto option
V8 4.0	3,950	94.0 x 71.0	190/4,750	236/3,000	9.34:1	R380	ZF HP22
V8 4.6	4,554	94.0 x 82.0	225/4,750	277/3,000	9.34:1	N/A	ZF HP24
Diesel							
2.5 4-cyl							
DT/DSE	2,497	80.0 x 82.8	134/4,400	199/2,300	22.0:1	R380	ZF HP22*

* Only manual gearbox available at time of launch.

ENGINES 1999–2002

Petrol	Capacity (cc)	Bore x stroke (mm)	Power bhp @ rpm	Torque lb ft @ rpm	Compression ratio	Manual gearbox	Auto option
V8 4.0	3,950	94.0 x 71.0	188/4,750	251/3,000	9.38:1	R380	ZF HP22
V8 4.6	4,554	94.0 x 82.0	218/4,750	295/3,000	9.37:1	N/A	ZF HP24
Diesel							
2.5 4-cyl							
DT/DSE	2,497	80.0 x 82.8	138/4,400	199/2,300	22.0:1	R380	ZF HP22

BRAKES

Front (in/mm)	11.7/297.2 diameter ventilated discs
Rear (in/mm)	12.0/304.0 diameter solid discs
ABS	four-channel anti-lock systems standard on all models
Parking brake	transmission brake drum on rear output from transfer

WHEELS AND TYRES

Construction	Alloy
Rim width	7J x 16 (8J x 16 on 4.6HSE model; optional on others)
Tyres	235/70 R16 105H
	255/65 R16 109H on 4.6HSE model; optional on others

VITAL STATISTICS

	V8 4.0-litre	V8 4.6-litre	Diesel 2.5-litre
EEC kerb weight (kg)** (models from 1944–99)	2,090 – manual 2,100 – auto	2,200 – auto only	2,115 – manual 2,130 – auto
Unladen weight (kg) (models from 1999–2002)	2,100 – auto only	2,230 – auto only	2,115 – manual 2,130 – auto

Wheelbase (mm)	2,745
Track front and rear (mm)	1,540/1,530
Overall length (mm)	4,713
Overall width (mm)	2,228
Overall height (mm)	1,817 (at standard ride height)
Max trailer towing weight (kg)	750 unbraked
	3,500 over-run brakes
Max gross vehicle weight (kg)	2,780

** All models: EEC Kerb weight is defined as the unladen weight plus a full tank of fuel plus a driver weighing 75kg.

Range Rover Series 3 (2002–)

ENGINES

Petrol	Capacity (cc)	Bore x stroke (mm)	Power bhp @ rpm	Torque lb ft @ rpm	Compression ratio	Transmission
V8 4.4	4,398	92.0x82.7	282/5,400	325/3,600	10:1	Electronic, dual mode, 5-speed automatic gearbox with Steptronic 2-speed chain-drive transfer box
Diesel						with Torsen centre differential
6-cyl 3.0	2,926	88.0x88.0	174/4,000	288/2,000	18:1	

VITAL STATISTICS

Unladen weight (kg)	2,440 (petrol) or 2,435 (diesel)
Wheelbase (mm)	2,880
Track front and rear (mm)	1,629/1,626
Overall length (mm)	4,950
Overall width (mm)	2,191
Height min/max (mm)	1,820/1,913
Max gross vehicle weight (kg)	3,050
Max trailer towing weight (kg)	750 unbraked – 3,500 over-run brakes

SUSPENSION

Front: cross-linked electronic air suspension with air struts

Rear: cross-linked electronic air suspension with double wishbones

All non-air suspension cars featured a Boge Hydromat self-levelling unit. Electronic air suspension was introduced on long wheelbase models from 1992.

BRAKES

Front diameter/width (mm)	344/30 ventilated discs
Rear diameter/width (mm)	354/12 solid discs
Parking brake	drum in rear disc, hand-lever operated
ABS system	Bosch 5.3

STEERING

Rack-and-pinion with Servotronic speed-sensitive assistance.

WHEELS AND TYRES

Wheels:	7.5J x 18 IS53, 5.5 x 19/IS49, 8.0J x 19/IS57
Tyres:	255/60R 18, 255/55R 19 (20in wheel/tyre combination optional)

The world's most capable vehicle. The Series 3 takes the Range Rover firmly into the future.

Appendix B

Numerology

Series 1

Originally, Range Rovers had chassis numbers in three different series depending on whether they were RHD home market, RHD export market or LHD export cars. Each series had its own three-figure prefix, as follows:

RHD home   355
RHD export   356
LHD export   358

The series 357 and 359 may have been allocated to CKD (completely knocked down) vehicles.

The following list shows the starting and finishing numbers in each of these three series from 1969 to approximately February 1975.

Year	355 RHD home	356 RHD export	358 LHD export
1969	355-00001 to -00003	None built	None built
1970	355-00004 to -00312	356-00001 to -00005	358-00001 to -00006
1971	355-00313 to -03157	356-00006 to -00068	358-00007 to -00745
1972	355-03158 to -05718	356-00069 to -00820	358-00746 to -03227
1973	355-05719 to -08659	356-00821 to -01857	358-03228 to -05837
1974	355-08660 to -10572	356-01858 to -03156	358-05838 to -09850
1975	355-10573 to -11062	356-03157 to -03292	358-09851 to -10556

In approximately February 1975, the system was changed so that all chassis numbers were issued in a common series for all specifications, but each individual vehicle was still given the distinctive prefix of 355, 356 or 358 as above, with CKD vehicles in the same sequence. From February 1975 to approximately October 1979, the starting and finishing numbers for each year were as follows:

Year	Chassis numbers
1975	355/356/358-12024 to -21662
1976	355/356/358-21663 to -31094
1977	355/356/358-31095 to -40479
1978	355/356/358-40480 to -55741
1979	355/356/358-55742 to -61821

The S1 VIN plate can be found under the bonnet riveted to the top of the front grille at the front of the engine compartment. The number is also stamped on the RH side of the chassis, forward of the spring mounting turret.

Key
A Type approval (UK only)
B VIN (max. 17 digits)
C Maximum permitted laden weight for vehicle
D Maximum vehicle and trailer weight
E Maximum road weight – front axle
F Maximum road weight – rear axle

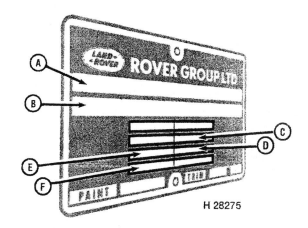

H 28275

VIN numbers

In approximately October 1979 (the start of the 1980 model year), the VIN (vehicle identification number) system was introduced. Each VIN plate, found on the front body crossmember, has an alpha-numeric, eight-character prefix, always starting with LH (for Land Rover marque and Range Rover model). Vehicles of all specifications share one series of numbers starting from 100001.

Starting and finishing numbers for each year were as follows:

Year	Chassis numbers
1979	100001 to 102163
1980	102164 to 110584
1981	110585 to 119702
1982	119703 to 131429
1983	131430 to 143040
1984	143041 to 154589
1985	154590 to 167941

From 1986, Land Rover changed the system and listed production totals, rather than start and finish chassis numbers.

Year	Chassis numbers
1986	14,494
1987	20,815
1988	24,021
1989	28,513
1990	24,202
1991	16,408
1992	15,334
1993	14,870
1994	15,283

Decoding the VIN prefix

The coding of VIN numbers and letters is explained here:-

1–2	(Post 1982 only) The first two letters are always SA which is the so-called World Manufacturer Identifier code. Here it's British Leyland or, later, the Rover Group Limited.
3	(Post 1982 only) This represents the division of the main manufacturer, i.e. Land Rover Limited.
4	The fourth letter is 'L' which stands for Land Rover.
5	'H' indicates the model range i.e. Range Rover.
6	Wheelbase: A is 100in / B is 108in
7	Number of doors: B is two-door / M is four-door / R is Monteverdi four-door
8	Engine type: E is VM Turbo diesel (2.4-litre) / F is Tdi Turbo diesel

L is V8 3.5-litre EFI
M is V8 3.8-litre EFI
N is VM Turbo diesel (2.5-litre)
V is V8 3.5-litre carburettor
3 is V8 4.2-litre EFI

9	Steering and transmission type:
	1 RHD four-speed manual
	2 LHD four-speed manual
	3 RHD automatic
	4 LHD automatic
	7 RHD five-speed manual
	8 LHD five-speed manual

10	Model year:	
	A	All models up to the end of the 1984 model year
	B	1985
	C	1984
	D	1985
	E	1986
	F	1987
	G	1988
	H	1989
	I	1990
	J	1991
	K	1992
	L	1993
	M	1994
	N	1995
	P	1996

11	Manufacturing plant:	
	A	Solihull UK
	F	Overseas (supplied as CKD)

All numbers following from this point constitute the actual serial number of the vehicle.

On Tdi diesel engines, the engine number is stamped on the RH side of the cylinder block above the camshaft front cover plate.

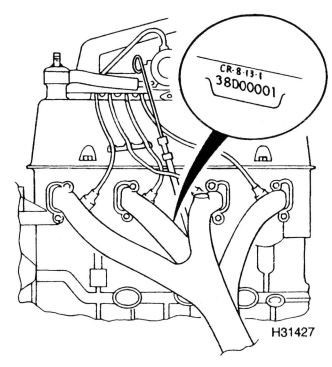

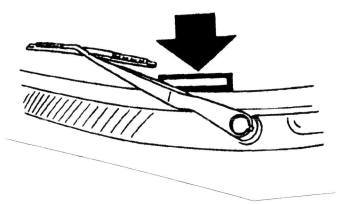

H31427

The engine number on V8 engines, is stamped onto a cast pad on the cylinder block on the LH top face in the centre, between cylinders three and five.

Series 2

The Series 2 has an adhesive label with the VIN number on it located on the LH side of the bonnet locking platform. It is also stamped on the outside of the chassis in the front RH wheel arch, to the rear of the anti-roll bar link.

SA VIN Number

An adhesive label with the VIN number, date of manufacture and gross front axle weight details is fitted to the lock face of the front LH door. Also included are wheel and tyre sizes and tyre pressures at gross axle weight ratings.

Decoding the VIN prefix

European code – S AL LP A M J 7 M A

S	Europe
AL	UK
LP	Range Rover
A	European specification
M	Four-door station wagon
J	4.6-litre fuel injection
7	Manual RHD steering
M	1995 model year
A	Solihull

USA code – S AL P V 1 2 4 2 S A

S	Europe
AL	UK
P	Range Rover
V	North American specification

On Series 2 Range Rovers the VIN is stamped on a plate which is visible through the LH side of the windscreen. (Land Rover Ltd)

1	Four-door station wagon
2	4-litre fuel injection
4	Automatic LHD drive steering
2	Check digit
S	1995 model year
A	Solihull

Engine numbers

The engine number on the 4.0 and 4.6-litre V8 engines is in the same position as shown in the previous diagram, on a cast pad on the cylinder block between cylinders three and five.

The BMW diesel engine has it stamped on the LH side of the cylinder block, above the sump.

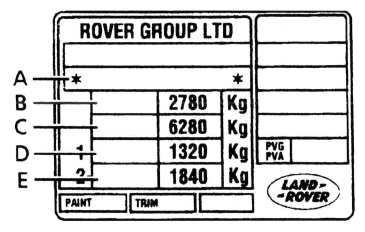

The plate you should find on a Series 2 Range Rover, with a key as follows:

A	VIN 17 digits
B	Maximum permitted laden weight for the vehicle
C	Maximum vehicle and trailer weight
D	Maximum road weight front axle
E	Maximum road weight rear axle

(Land Rover Ltd)

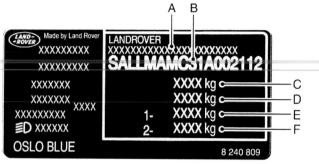

This is the Series 3 VIN plate, with a key as follows:

A   Type approval *

B   VIN number

C   Gross vehicle weight *

D   Gross train weight *

E   Maximum front axle load *

F   Maximum rear axle load *

        * Where required.

(Land Rover Ltd)

Series 3

The VIN number, together with maximum vehicle weights, is stamped on a plate riveted to the top of the LH front suspension tower in the engine bay. In addition, it is also stamped on a plate visible through the lowest part of the left side of the windscreen. It is also stamped on the vehicle body on the front face of the RH front suspension tower, in the engine bay.

The story so far. After three generations, the Range Rover continues to set the benchmark for off-road ability combined with on-road excellence.

Technical information

Car manufacturers and aftermarket suppliers regularly mix and match terminology which combines with the UK's gradual conversion from imperial to metric to make it increasingly tricky for the Range Rover owner to get a total grip on what's what. This simple conversion table will help to ensure that you get it right every time.

To convert	To	Multiply by
Length		
inches	millimetres	25.4
millimetres	inches	0.0394
miles	kilometres	1.609
kilometres	miles	0.621
Volume		
cubic inches	cubic centimetres	16.387
cubic centimetres	cubic inches	0.061
Imperial gallons	litres	4.546
litres	Imperial gallons	0.22
Weight		
pounds	kilograms	0.454
kilograms	pounds	2.205
Speed		
mph	kph	1.609
kph	mph	0.621
Fuel consumption		
Imperial mpg	litre per 100km	divide mpg figure into 283
litres per 100km	Imperial mpg	2.825

Bolt identification, metric/Imperial and thread sizes

When it comes to sorting out bolt identification, look for an 'S' or an 'R' stamped on the head, which denotes that it is Imperial.

Imperial threads per inch (TPI)

	4BA	2BA	No. 10	$1/4$in	$5/16$in	$3/8$in	$7/16$in
BA	38.5	31.4					
UNC			24	20	18	16	14
UNF			32	28	24	24	20
BSF				26	22	20	18
BSW				20	18	16	14

The figure 8.8 on the head shows that it is a metric bolt. The threads on imperial fasteners are shown as threads per inch (TPI). On metric bolts, the pitch is the length of ten threads. So, a bolt described as M10 x 1.5 pitch, is one with a shank diameter of 10mm where ten threads cover a distance of 1.5cm. This table shows the pitches used on most* metric bolts

Bolt size	Pitch (mm)
M5	0.8
M6	1.00
M8	1.25
M10	1.5
M12	1.75

* For some reason, the pitch on Japanese 10mm bolts is a finer, 1.25, rather than the usual 1.5.

Useful contacts

As well as the postal address and telephone number for each company, the e-mail and website address have also been included where available. If you are buying 'online', it is important to ensure that the site is 'secure' and that your credit card details cannot be stolen by a third party. In addition, we would not recommend any Internet connection or E-mail communication without some form of anti-virus protection to inhibit potentially dangerous computer 'bugs' getting on to your machine and wreaking havoc. A personal 'firewall' should prevent computer hackers breaking and entering your machine and stealing card and PIN numbers etc. All addresses and sites were correct at the time of writing but are subject to change.

Ashcroft Transmissions Ltd

Unit 8, Titan Court, Laporte Way, Luton, Beds, LU4 8EF
01582 750400
E-mail: dave@ashcrofttrans.ndo.co.uk
Website: www.ashcroft-transmissions.co.uk
Range Rover manual and automatic gearbox specialists.

Autoleads

Unit 80, Woolmer Trading Estate, Bordon, Hants, GU35 9QF
01420 476767
E-mail: info@autoleads.co.uk
Website: www.autoleads.co.uk
All manner of ICE accessories and adaptors to make connecting new items of non-original sound equipment easy.

Bailcast Ltd

Unit 8, Chorley North Industrial Park, Chorley, Lancashire, PR6 7BX
01257 266060

E-mail: enquiry@bailcast.com
Website: www.bailcast.com
Producers of neoprene rubber swivel housing gaiters for all Range Rovers up to 1995.

Brightwells

Country Vehicle Auctions, A49 By-pass, Leominster, Herefordshire. HR6 8NZ
01568 611166
E-mail: vehicles@brightwells.com
Website: www.brightwells.com
Auctioneers with a regular 4x4 auction where you can always find a large selection of Range Rovers

Burlen Fuel Systems Ltd

Spitfire House, Castle Road, Salisbury, Wilts, SP1 3SA
01722 412500
E-mail: info@burlen.co.uk
Website: www.burlen.co.uk
SU and Stromberg carburettors sales and spares.

Carflow

See Evo.

Car Parts Direct

160 Burton Road, Derby, DE1 1TN
01332 290833
E-mail: sales@carparts-direct.co.uk
Website: www.carparts-direct.co.uk
All kinds of maintenance parts and accessories, including the highly rated Rossini drilled and grooved brake discs.

Clarke International

Hemnal Street, Epping, Essex, CM16 4LG
01992 565300

E-mail: clarkeint@aol.com
All kinds of hand tools and pneumatic machinery and tools, work benches, etc.

Dakar Cars Ltd
Stanhill Farm, Birchwood Road, Dartford, Kent, DA2 7HD
01322-614044
E-mail: sales@dakar.co.uk
Website: www.dakar.co.uk/index2.htm
Range Rover servicing, modification and production of the Range Rover-based Dakar kit car.

Department of Transport (DETR), Public Enquiries Unit
0207 890 3333
All matters relating to vehicle/roads legislation and the environment.

Eberspächer (UK) Ltd
Headlands Business Park, Salisbury Road, Ringwood, Hants, BH24 3PB
01425 480151
E-mail: enquiries@eberspacher.com
Website: www.eberspacher.com
Manufacturers of diesel and petrol engine vehicle heating systems including the Hydronic pre-heater, ideal for Range Rover V8 or diesel engines.

Evo Automotive Solutions
Unit 7, Denbigh Hall, Milton Keynes, MK3 7QT
01908 646566
Suppliers of top quality Evo/Carflow locking wheel bolts to suit Range Rover steel or alloy wheels.

Jeremy J Fearn
Fold Farm, Beeley, Nr Matlock, Derbyshire DE4 2NQ
01629 732546
E-mail: jjf.interoolers@btinternet.com
Website: www.jjf.intercoolers.btinternet.co.uk
Diesel specialist supplying and fitting chip uprates and larger interoolers for increased power, torque and mpg.

Garmin (Europe) Ltd
Unit 5, The Quadrangle, Abbey Park, Romsey, Hants, SO51 9AQ
01794 519944
Website: www.garmin.com
Producers of a whole range of portable satellite navigation devices, ideal for the Range Rover owner,

whether going off into the wilderness or delving the depths of Deptford.

Gordon Finlay
Woolcombes, Newton Poppleford, Sidmouth, Devon, EX10 0DF
01395 568488 (mobile: 07974 397227)
LPG installation expert, supply and installation service of Iwema equipment, with bases in Devon and Cambridgeshire.

Goodyear Great Britain Ltd
Stafford Road, Wolverhampton, West Midlands, WV10 6DH
01902 327000
Website: www.goodyear.co.uk
Wide range of quality on-road/off-road/in-between tyres designed specifically for the Range Rover, fitted on some models as standard.

The Heritage Motor Centre
Banbury Road, Gaydon, Warwicks, CV35 0BJ
01926 641188
E-mail: clubs@heritagemotorcentre.org.uk
Website: www.heritage.org.uk
Repository of British motoring history, including many interesting and unique Range Rovers.

Holley Carburettors
See RPi Engineering.

Iwema Enterprise
Duinbeek 3, 5653PL Eindhoven, Holland
0(031) 40 252 3950
E-mail: iwema.lpg@chello.nl
Website: www.iwemaenterprise.nl
LPG conversions specialists, with a wide range of kits and components for all Range Rover models including diesel. Producers of a very useful handbook of LPG installation. (See also Gordon Finlay, Chris Perfect.)

Kenlowe Limited
Burchetts Green, Maidenhead, Berks, SL6 6QU
01628 823303
E-mail: sales@kenlowe.com
Website: www.kenlowe.com
Electric fan kits to replace original viscous version and hot-start warm up device, both designed to aid efficiency and improve mpg.

Landcraft, David Mitchell's
Plas Yn Dre, High Street, Bala, Gwynedd, LL23 7LU
01678 520820/07050 664374
Off-road courses in the beautiful Welsh mountains, off-road training and a huge range of 4x4 models.

Land Rover UK Limited
Land Rover UK, Warwick Technology Park, Warwick,
CV34 6RG
08705 000 500
Website: www.landrover.com
Range Rover manufacturer.

L.E.G.S.
Units 2 & 3 Mile Oak Industrial Estate, Maesbury Road,
Oswestry, Shropshire, SY10 8GA
01691 653737/01691 671444
E-mail: sales@legs.co.uk
Website: www.legs.co.uk
Manual transmission specialist reconditioners, including gearboxes, transfer boxes, differentials, with one or two-year warranty. Also rebuilt 200 Tdi engines. Parts and mail order service.

M.A.D. Suspension
Unit 13, Harrier Park, Didcot, Oxon, OX11 7PL
01235 511494
E-mail: info@mad-suspension.com
Website: www.mad-suspension.com
The interactive suspension 'airbag' system which utilises an on-board pneumatic pump to raise and lower rear springs to compensate for extra loads and/or large trailer weights.

McDonald Landrover Ltd
Unit 18, Mile Oak Industrial Estate, Maesbury Road,
Oswestry, Shropshire, SY10 8HA
01691 657705
E-mail: rupert@mcdonaldlandrover.co.uk
Website: www.mcdonaldlandrover.co.uk
Spares, accessories, service, LPG fitting and just about everything for the Range Rover enthusiast.

McGard
Smarter Direct Marketing Ltd, Parsonage Farm, Penn,
Bucks, HP10 8PE
01494 817080
E-mail: info@smarterdirect.com
Website: www.mcgard.com
Manufacturers of excellent quality, award-winning Ultra

High Security locking wheel nuts suitable for both alloy and steel wheels.

MetaSystem UK Ltd
Oakmore Court, Kingswood Road, Hampton Lovett,
Droitwich, Worcs, WR9 0QH
01905 791700
E-mail: info@metasystem.co.uk
Websites: www.metaystem.co.uk and www.smartire.com
Automotive security specialists, Targa SR2 reversing aid and SmarTire electronic pressure checking/warning system for all models.

Nationwide Trim
Unit 17, West Washford Industrial Area, Redditch, Worcs,
B98 0DG
01527 518851
Website: www.nationwidetrim.demon.co.uk
Suppliers of all items of Range Rover trim from a door panel to a complete refurbishment, as featured in the 'Interiors' section of this book. Leather interiors a speciality.

Overfinch Bespoke Vehicles
Unit 8, Farnham Trading Estate, Farnham, Surrey, GU9
9NQ
01252 731950
E-mail: info@overfinch.com
Website: www.overfinch.co.uk
Choose from Range Rover, Discovery or Defender product ranges then, let Overfinch mechanically and/or cosmetically enhance the vehicle to your own exacting requirements.

Paddock Spares and Accessories
The Showground, The Cliff, Matlock, Derbyshire,
ED4 5EW
01629 584499
E-mail: sales@paddockspares.com
Website: www.paddockspares.com
Mail-order service offering all manner of spares, accessories and maintenance items to keep your Range Rover happy without spending a fortune.

Chris Perfect Components
Pant y Nos, Cellan, Lampeter, Ceredigion, Wales,
SA48 8HL
01570 423206
E-mail: sales@chrisperfect.com
Website: www.chrisperfect.com

LPG installation expert, supply and installation service of Iwema equipment, specialising in carburettor engines.

Pharmhouse Marketing (Mark Adams)
01694 720 143 (mobile 07798 582390)
E-mail: mark.adams@bjds.com
An independent specialist for more than ten years working only with Rover V8 engine management, fuel injection and ignition systems. New, remanufactured and used parts, standard or uprated. Support for vehicles with catalytic converters by Lambda Correction Analysis. Computerised 4WD rolling roads and engine dyna-mometer available to set-up and diagnose any vehicle.

RH Engineering
Clywedog Road South, Wrexham Industrial Estate, Wrexham, LL13 9XS
01978 664316
E-mail: sales@polybush.co.uk
Website: www.polybush.co.uk
Long-lasting Polybush polyurethane suspension bushes to replace the original rubber versions. Better handling and long-term performance, in 'softer' standard format and original 'harder' classic versions.

Rimmer Brothers Ltd
Sleaford Road, Triumph House, Bracebridge Heath, Lincoln, LN4 2NA
01522 568000
E-mail: sales@rimmerbros.co.uk
Website: www.rimmerbros.co.uk
Sales of Classic and S2 cars plus a complete range of Range Rover products from engines to wheel bolts and including their famous range of standard/sports stainless steel exhaust systems and Polybush suspension bushes. Comprehensive free catalogue available.

Roof Box Company, The
Unit 1A, Toll Bar Estate, Sedbergh, Cumbria, LA10 5HA
08700 766326
Website: www.roofbox.co.uk
Range of roofboxes, cycle carriers, bootliners and Walser waterproof seat covers, all ideal for the Range Rover enthusiast.

RPi Engineering
Wayside Garage, Holt Road, Horsford, Norwich, Norfolk, NR10 3EE
01603 891209
E-mail: rpi@rpiv8.com

Website: www.v8engines.com
Rover V8 engine specialists, rebuilding to original specification, tuned or new capacity. Also, custom-designed V8 LPG conversions. Valuable contributors to this book and the fount of all Rover V8 knowledge.

SIP (Industrial Products Ltd)
Gelders Hall Road, Shepshed, Loughborough, Leics, LE12 9NH
01509 503141
E-mail: info@sip-group.com
Website: www.sip-group.com
High-quality DIY/professional welding equipment, portable generators and air tools.

SmarTire
See MetaSystem UK.

SU Carburettors
See Burlen.

Teng Tools
Unit 5, Flitwick Industrial Estate, Maulden Road, Flitwick, Beds, MK45 1UF
01525 718080
Website: www.tengtools.co.uk
Importers of Teng's range of high-quality hand tools.

Thatcham
Colthrop Lane, Thatcham, Newbury, Berks, RG19 4NP
01635 868855
E-mail: enquiries@thatcham.org
Website: www.thatcham.org
The insurance industry testing body. The fitting of an approved device helps safeguard your Range Rover and can lead to insurance discounts.

van Aaken Developments Ltd
Crowthorne Business Centre, Telford Avenue, Crowthorne, Berks, RG45 6XA
01344 777553
E-mail: vanaaken@vanaaken.com
Website: www.vanaaken.com
Electronic tuning for both petrol and diesel engines using 'Smart' chips and 'black box' technology.

VSIB (Vehicle Security Installation Board)
Bates Business Centre, Church Road, Harold Wood, Romford, Essex, RM3 0JF
01708 340911

E-mail: E-mail@vsib.co.uk

Website: www.vsib.co.uk

The National Regulatory and Accreditation body for Vehicle Systems Installers and their installations.

Wakefield Storage Handling Ltd

Radford Road, New Basford, Nottingham, NG7 7EF

0115 854 1000

Importers of top-quality, Equipto benches and workshop storage equipment.

The Walnut Dash Company

17 Church Road, Great Bookham, Leatherhead, Surrey, KT23 3PG

01372 415659

E-mail: sales@walnutdash.fsnet.co.uk

Website: www.walnutdash.fsnet.co.uk

Suppliers of high-quality, self-adhesive precision-cut walnut interior trim complete with a ten-year warranty. Also repairs of existing wooden trim.

Graham Whitehouse

Brooklands House, Nimmings Road, Halesowen, West Midlands, B62 9JE

0121 559 9800

E-mail: info@gwautos.com

Website: www.gwautos.com

Chrysler automatic gearbox and torque converter specialists; all types of conversion undertaken.

Specialist magazines

Land Rover Owner

Land Rover Owner International, EMAP Automotive Ltd, Media House, Lynchwood, Peterborough Business Park, Peterborough PE2 6EA UK

01733 468231

Website: www.lromagazine.com

Land Rover World/Off Road and 4-wheel drive

IPC Focus Network, 9 Dingwall Avenue, Croydon, Surrey, CR9 2TA

020 8774 0600

Website: www.ipc.co.uk

Land Rover Monthly

Priory Cottage, Geeding, Suffolk, IP30 0QE

01359 240066

E-mail: editorial@lrm.co.uk

Website: www.lrm.co.uk

Land Rover Enthusiast

PO Box 178, Wallingford DO, Oxfordshire, OX10 8PD

01491 202522

E-mail: editorial@landroverenthusiast.com

Website: www.landroverenthusiast.com

Clubs and organisations

Camel Trophy Owners Club

Holly Simm, Bendrose Corner, Finch Lane, Amersham Common, Bucks, HP7 9LU

E-mail: ctoc_secretary@cameltrophy.org

Website: www.cameltrophy.org

Range Rover Register

Nigel Webster, The Elms, Abbey Road, Revesby, Boston, Lincs, PE22 7NX

E-mail: membership.secretary@rrr.co.uk

Website: www.rrr.co.uk

Index